FRIED FLOWERS AND FANGO

A love affair with an old Italian spa town

Myra Robinson

authorHOUSE®

AuthorHouse™ UK Ltd.
500 Avebury Boulevard
Central Milton Keynes, MK9 2BE
www.authorhouse.co.uk
Phone: 08001974150

First published by AuthorHouse 2/28/2011

ISBN: 978-1-4520-9773-2

This book is printed on acid-free paper.

For all my family, in the hope that my grandchildren, Freddy, Archie, Stan, Milo, Harry and Matilda, will grow up loving Italy as much as I do.

Contents

FRIED FLOWERS AND FANGO:

a love affair with an old Italian spa town

"Don't be so stupid," said the man in my life dismissively when I suggested on impulse that I might blow all my savings on a little place in Italy.

"It'll be freezing in winter." (It is.)

"It'll be ridiculously complicated." (It was.)

"You'll get tired of always staying in the same place." (I don't.)

"You don't speak the language." (I do now.)

1. HOT WATER AND A DOZEN WAYS TO COOK A RABBIT

"No, signora. You don't want to stay here. This *albergo* isn't for tourists. Try one of the other spa towns in the hills."

A hotel not for tourists? What kind of a place was this?

"But do you have a room?" I persisted.

He didn't seem to understand that it was precisely because the town of Montebello was sleepy and not full of tourists that I wanted to stay. He was pretty sleepy himself: we'd had to wake him, slumped over the desk, to ask for a room.

"I only have a room without air conditioning and it's very hot. *Molto caldo.*" He shook his head sadly.

We said we'd take it. If we survived the challenge of an overnight stay without air conditioning, we reasoned that he might then let us have a better room.

After a near-obsession with visiting spa towns, first in France, and when these were exhausted, Italy, I had finally fetched up in a faded backwater once renowned as having the best mud in Italy.

This was the fateful encounter which began my love affair with Italian spa establishments, especially those which have seen better days. When I think about it, it was an encounter that changed my life. In fact, I wouldn't be writing this book now if I hadn't stayed there, and all the stories which follow are a direct consequence of suffering that first hot and sweaty night in Montebello. My partner Phil decided to sleep in the bath where it was marginally cooler, but we weathered the endurance test. We stayed in that little non-tourist hotel and others like it for several summers, each time becoming more amazed and bewildered by what went on.

There are spa towns with thermal pools all over Italy. Many are grand stylish resorts, important tourist destinations where they hold *Miss Italia* competitions (Salsomaggiore), open air rock concerts (Montecatini Terme) or Verdi operas (Abano Terme). These major ones are rather like Cecil B. de Mille film sets, where waters emerge in formal steaming pools surrounded by pseudo classical Greek columns, or through elaborate taps in the form of lions' mouths. At Montecatini the taps are of increasing salinity: the doctor tells you at which tap to begin to take the waters, and you move along the row. Unsurprisingly, there's a row of discreet lavatories at the far end.

Other Italian spa towns have different quirky attractions, but are no less grand. Monsumato Terme near Pistoia is famous for its spa treatment in steaming hot caves. In Fiuggi there is a spring which, they claim, combines diuretic properties with an ability to dissolve kidney stones and prevent them re-forming. At Tivoli the waters gush out from two lakes and are still known by their Roman name, the Acque Albule. The water appears to be thick and creamy because of the gassy froth which forms on its surface. This was thought to be a miraculous panacea in Roman times, and even today, wealthy *curisti* from Rome flock there for treatments of the respiratory system, but as they go year after year, it can hardly be regarded as a cure.

Then there are the small faded spas which had their peak around the 1930s to 50s when a "cure" was probably the only holiday an ordinary Italian family would have. These little places still cling to their genteel past with hotels and pools which have seen better days but which attract the same families year after year. After all, they tell me, the curative properties of the water and mud haven't changed. It is these shabby little spa towns which I love, and which have persuaded me to come back year after year, just as the Italians do, to immerse myself literally and metaphorically in taking the waters.

The thermal pools are always outdoors and fed by naturally hot bubbling springs. In summer they are often unpleasant in the heat of the day, rather like swimming in warm Alka Seltzer. In my favourite area of thermal springs, the Euganean Hills, there are 240 thermal pools. The water comes out of the ground under pressure after a journey of over 100 miles at a temperature of 87 degrees centigrade.

There is usually a fine line to be drawn between what is an acceptable water temperature and what is *troppo freddo* (too cold) or *troppo caldo* (too hot). 33 degrees is about right. When the floating thermometer shows 35 or more there are protests to the *padrone* with demands to top it up with ordinary cold water. At 31, this same ever-obliging individual is sought out to open up the valves and let more naturally hot water in. We *inglesi* find swimming in hot fizzy bath water rather fatiguing, but we have to bow to their experience in these matters.

Scattered about the volcanic hills are a few ordinary swimming pools which proudly advertise that they are full of COLD WATER. This is a great selling point in the heat of summer when there's a need to feel cooler.

In winter the pools create hovering cubes of steam above them, with spots of colour which can be identified as swimming hats bobbing about here and there. I love the oddly satisfying feeling of beginning to swim a length in a small indoor pool, entering a wide tunnel with strips of plastic at the end, then swimming through to greet the outdoors, with trees covered in frost, and chickens pecking around the edges of frozen puddles. No one gets out of the water. If you stand up and expose your shoulders you realise how cold the air is. You can't see far through the steam, but the misty haze gives a romantic soft-focus view of the pine trees whilst obscuring the worst excesses of concrete functional architecture.

Each pool has its own group of faithful *clienti*, returning year after year on the same week from all corners of Italy, and behaving like one big family. It took us about three years to become a part of the *Second Week in August Family* at Montebello, but now we are included in every crazy thing they do. If the Man With No Voice (- just how do you cure a malfunctioning larynx with mud?) decides we should have an ice cream after dinner, we *all* go. We trustingly follow him in convoy to the best *gelateria* over a couple of hills with several hairpin bends, despite the fact that he's already had a litre of the local *vino* and a grappa before setting out. I slightly disapprove of him, since everybody knows that his wife stays behind in Milan whilst he turns up each year with a different *signora,* but he's great fun and provides perfect material for gossiping in the pool.

La Stupenda arrives each year from Trieste, mute hen-pecked husband in tow, and regales us with salacious goings-on. The women stand round her, waist deep in the shallow end, anxious to know who the cook's sleeping with this year, (one of the waiters, usually) and who will inherit the *albergo*. Mostly these elderly women can't swim, but that isn't the point. They take their exercise by clutching the edge of the pool and pulling themselves gingerly all the way round, or else they occasionally put on inflated arm bands and flap about in the shallow end with appropriate encouragement, but they prefer to soak their legs and gossip, issuing throaty chuckles and exclamations of "*Mamma mia!*" and "*Da vero!*"

But on Sundays *La Stupenda* sings at mass in the local *chiesa* and we're all expected to give moral support. Rumour has it that she once attended a master class with Maria Callas. Now what she lacks in accuracy she makes up for in power and we leave the church with ears ringing.

Rules and customs must be observed. Everyone has to wear a *cuffia*, a nylon swimming cap which neither keeps the hair dry nor stays on the head. All bathers must walk through the foot bath – it's the only way into the pool. There are ingenious ways of avoiding this, though. Most people can't jump over it, but instead do a balancing act along the railings on either side. Showers have to be taken before and after swimming. The women all follow the same procedure when they leave the pool. First their hair is carefully rinsed, then expertly coiled inside a turban. Then for the next 20 minutes they hang their heads upside down combing through their hair with their fingers whilst the sun dries it. Could this be an instinctive modern version of the eighteenth century Venetian ladies' habit of spreading out their hair on specially designed roof balconies to bleach in the sun? I don't know, but I like to think so.

These days, young Italian families aren't much interested in traditional spas, which tend to be populated by the late middle-aged and elderly. The shops in the spa towns reflect their clientele. In ChiancianoTerme there's a shop which supplies trusses and corsets for short plump elderly men. It is the models in this shop which are particularly appealing. Probably dating from the 1940s, they are tubby jolly little men who are laughing, not just smiling or looking out with the hauteur of 21st century mannequins. They display all sorts of curious contraptions for supporting and controlling parts of the body, but which are clearly enjoyable to wear. We were so taken with this display that we photographed it, to the great disapproval of a couple hobbling past on their zimmer frames.

You get the picture: a slower pace of life for the elderly but not quite past it. The bonus is that you're always likely to be amongst the youngest people in the resort.

The happy invalids taking the cure spend their time limping, shuffling and staggering from mud bath to dining room to bedroom (siesta) and bedroom to pool, very convenient for the mad dogs and Englishmen who in consequence have a whole swimming pool to themselves from 12.30 to 3.30 every day.

But it's not half as much fun as when they all re-emerge to dunk themselves for another three hours with more pool-side conversation. An elderly blonde woman who wore a different pair of Dame Edna-type sun glasses every day in the pool and, they whispered, had sacks of money, showed me some small flecks of white on her tanned leathery legs.

"This is shameful," she complained. "They put scalding mud on my legs and this is the result."

Personally, I found it hard to believe. If you're covered from neck to toes in mud, how can you get minute specks of scalding? Her part in the competition for most interesting ailments was to let everyone know that she has plastic knees. Others have more mundane problems like arthritis or rheumatism.

Overheard at the pool on another hot afternoon: (even if the topic is very personal, they never lower their voices.)

"Mamma mia, how humid it is today! I'm sweating. Need to go for a swim."

"No, you can't. It's too soon after eating. You need to rest for three hours."

"I never used to sweat like this, even after the gym. But after the menopause I sweat like crazy."

At this point the Elvis couple clambered along the railings to avoid the footbath and joined us. I called them the Elvis couple because they both wore white studded shorts, lots of gold jewellery, and white shirts with the collars turned up. Mr Elvis had his hair in a shiny black pompadour, of course. Mrs Elvis, who had the largest pair of gold hoop earrings I've ever seen, and carried a transistor radio like a handbag, wore a leopard skin bikini under her whites. They had an elaborate ritual for their comfort and convenience after the lunchtime siesta. They lined up ash trays, packets of cigarettes, glasses and a bottle of *prosecco* in a cooler, and tiny foam cups of espresso along the edge of the pool, then gently lowered themselves into the water, being careful not to wet their coiffures. Smoking and drinking whilst immersed, they could now join in the general chat, or listen to Euro pop on their radio.

The endlessly fascinating topic of food is the number one subject of pool-side conversation. The best way to cook rabbit can last for an hour or more, even leading to heated arguments. Roast or stewed? Which herbs should be used? Can you make a pasta sauce with it? (The locals say you can only do that with hares.)

Some of the matrons are occasionally coaxed into giving away secrets when they're feeling particularly expansive in the warm relaxing bubbles.

"Did you know that if you add a spoonful of water to a *soffritto* of chopped onion it will stop you burping?" Marisa confides to her cronies.

Italians love titles and use them at every opportunity. At first I found it very impressive that in ordinary little hotels we were often surrounded by *dottore* and *professore*. One evening I found myself sitting next to a man everyone addressed as *Presidente.* He was flatteringly attentive, topping up my *prosecco* far more often than I'd realised, with the result that the next day I paid the price and was confined to my bed. The hotel guests were angry with him for causing my hangover, and made him write a note of apology which he pushed under the bedroom door. With it was his business card. He was the president of the section of motorway between Bologna and Florence, and offered me life-long breakdown cover on his stretch of road.

The owners of small spa hotels like to point out with pride the small touches they make each year to improve facilities. In Salice Terme one *albergo* owner has created a few new bathrooms, all-in-one plastic pod arrangements rather like aeroplane lavatories, to be entered by an "artistic" hole in the wall. This is a man who enjoys novelty. He also enjoys showing off his voluptuous blonde Russian wife who, rather like Valentina in *A History of Tractors in Ukranian,* enjoys life in the West without actually doing anything much beyond looking decorative.

In the Euganean Hills where time-travelling back to the 50s continues, especially in Montebello, additional touches are less dramatic: new parasols, pots of geraniums on the stairs at the entrance, or a new gaudy flower bed which never survives the summer heat.

My favourite *albergo* has a mat at the entrance on which the name appears, flanked by two stars. Rather endearingly, someone has taken the trouble to cut out and sew on an additional star in the middle, though I doubt very much whether it's officially rated as three star.

Signor Bianco, the manager, is in his 80s, a tiny man who like the dormouse in *Alice in Wonderland* spends most of his time asleep over his desk. He keeps the takings in a shoe box next to him: anyone could walk off with thousands of euros, but of course no one ever does.

Opposite his sleeping form is the entrance to the dining room where there is frequently a cluster of people jostling to see what's on the day's menu. The doors to the dining room are closed, with a curtain in front which is dramatically swished aside as the head waiter, Matteo, makes the announcement "*Signori, signore, è pronto la cena,*" (Ladies and Gentlemen, dinner is served) at which point the crowd surges forward for pole position at the antipasti buffet.

Signor Bianco has his own table in the dining room, near the entrance to the kitchen. On his table is an impressive line-up of bottles and packets of medication, parallel with the oil and vinegar, salt and pepper, toothpicks, the dish which contains parmesan cheese, and other paraphernalia. Everyone nods courteously at him on entering the room, and he acknowledges them regally, meanwhile preparing for his great daily gastronomic performance of cheese-eating. He takes a teaspoon which he then shovels into the bowl of parmesan. With a dextrous flick of the wrist, a stream of grated cheese flies through the air into his mouth without a single spill. This he repeats until he is served with his first course. Not for him the competition around the antipasti buffet. He has his salad brought to him, usually before he has managed to empty the dish of parmesan.

Breakfast was a puzzling experience the first time we stayed in that same little hotel. I was rather surprised to discover that at breakfast people shuffled in wearing towelling dressing gowns, mainly grubby white ones, but occasionally in pastel colours. My brightly-coloured cotton sun dress stuck out like a sore thumb. But there was worse to come. Modesty is not a high priority: clearly no one bothers to wear anything beneath.

"Have you noticed that we're the only people here who are dressed?" I whispered to Phil as we sat down in the dining room. I didn't mention the part view of a man's privates opposite me. He wasn't a flasher: he was unconcernedly buttering his morning bread roll whilst his wrap fell open, revealing all.

I have learned not to look at other diners, knowing all too well what might creep into view if the belt from a towelling wrap slips undone. My first impressions of the spotless tablecloths and smart *clienti* had taken a nosedive, but of course I now know that it's because they've either just come upstairs from their mud treatment, or have appointments straight after breakfast, and this involves being totally naked and encased in hot mud for whatever length of time it says on your prescription. (As I describe in chapter 2.) And the mud gets everywhere, no matter how hard you try to keep it off your clothes.

* * *

Most traditional spa towns are small, and, like Montebello, tucked away in attractive hilly landscapes. Bagno di Romagna is such a place, half way between Perugia and Ravenna. Mud is not always on the menu here, but there are other curative delights such as can be seen on the not-very-alluring local postcard with its shots of the apparatus for exercising leg muscles, and the curious contraption for intimate torture, the gynaecological irrigation machine. Whether it's with mud or not is anybody's guess, but I wouldn't be prepared to risk it; nor a nasal douche, especially not 3rd class.

Life in Bagno di Romagna has the usual routines of gentle walks up and down the only shopping street, sitting on the benches in the shady park, and taking drinks which last for hours at the couple of cafes, or at the kiosk in the park, where they keep the key to the only public lavatories.

Sometimes, at great sacrifice if they're staying on a full board basis, the visitors will choose to have a freshly made *piadina* for lunch. The little shop has a pile of dough behind the counter, from which the obliging girl pulls off a chunk and kneads it thoroughly before rolling it into a ball. This is then put through a kind of stainless steel mangle to squash it into a disc. Below the rollers is a smaller version of the mangle which by turning the handle produces a paper-thin flat circle to be cooked on a hot plate then filled with one of at least 30 fillings. There's also a sealed version, *crescioni*, like a flatter (and far nicer) version of a Cornish pasty. I can recommend *piadine* to anyone looking for a delicious light lunch in central Italy.

And here we come full circle, to return to the first love of all Italians, food. Not only does the topic of food occupy almost every waking moment of all *curisti* (or indeed all Italians); it is also a source of great delight to go to a spa town not in one's own region, so as to try the local specialities and then declare them not to be as good as at home, all debate naturally taking place in the pool. If you happen to come from Naples, *piadine* are of course nowhere near as good as an honest pizza. If you regularly enjoy the cuisine of the Veneto, you will complain about the lack of *bigoli* (a kind of thick spaghetti) with duck meat sauce in the spa towns of Umbria. The hot water spa of Acqui Terme of course has better wines than its equivalent further south, Saturnia, because it's near the Langhe, famous for its *dolcetto, barbera,* and above all *barolo* wines.

A few years ago the Italian government tried to do away

with the idea that Italians could spend a week or more each year having a cure on their National Health Service, a sort of free holiday. There was almost a national riot. Spas are part of a way of life which essentially goes back to Roman times. If they have lasted so long, there is no likelihood of their imminent demise.

2. FANGO: MUD, GLORIOUS MUD.

We had realised on our first morning at what became our favourite "three star" *albergo* in Montebello that something strange, mysterious and possibly sinister happened at dawn every day. We were woken by a clanking, whirring and sloshing noise which for days we couldn't explain.

Eventually, straying into a cordoned-off area beyond the pool which bubbled up warm and fizzy, like effervescent soup straight from the underground source, we found ourselves looking over several ponds of gently bubbling chocolate-coloured mud. Rather like giant food mixers, huge blades were steadily rotating, keeping the gloopy mixture smooth. Around the edges, trolleys and carts were stacked with buckets, and a drying area was hung with large flapping black rubber mats. It all looked rather sinister.

A bulky fellow guest, all body and very little head, came towards us gesticulating and shouting for us to get out of the place. He reminded me of Bluto, but as I'm no Olive Oyle, and Phil doesn't eat spinach, we retreated. He patrolled the area regularly, we discovered, as if the whole set-up were top secret. Resolving to keep out of Bluto's way, we called a temporary halt to our investigations. (Though eventually Bluto became a friend, whose real name turned out to be Massimo. You'll meet him in chapter 5.)

A few days later we joined in the conversation about cures in the dining room.

"Best mud in Italy," a fellow guest claimed at lunchtime when we asked about it. Intrigued, I decided I had to try the treatment. After all, we're always reading in magazines about costly trendy spas, and they were getting all this on their National Health. They all swore by it, although as they all came back year after year, it hardly seemed to be a cure.

A couple of years and 40 Italian lessons later, I ventured to ask Signor Bianco, the ancient sleepy hotel manager, if I could have mud treatment. (I'd learned that the Italian word for mud was, improbably, *fango.)*

"What's wrong with you?" he asked.

I was foolish enough to say, "Nothing".

"In that case, signora" he sighed, shaking his head, "you do not need a mud cure."

I don't like being thwarted. The following year, I asked again. This time, I had a plan of campaign. Back pain would, it seemed to me, guarantee all-over treatment whilst not being specific enough for them to detect that it wasn't true.

I was allocated an appointment with the visiting doctor the following day. It was a difficult consultation. The doctor had clearly had a stroke, and only spoke from one side of his mouth.

My limited knowledge of Italian didn't stretch to this kind of situation, but with a great deal of concentration and with the aid of a diagram of a female body and a dictionary, we came to an understanding of sorts. I explained my constant back trouble and submitted myself to examination. After taking my blood pressure and listening to my heart, and after I'd responded to lots of questions instinctively with a "yes" or "no" depending on his tone of voice, he seemed persuaded.

"Yes, signora" he agreed. "You will need six buckets of mud for four days."

This prescription, worded exactly as he'd said, was written with a flourish and handed to me, the passport to an unforgettable and possibly life-threatening experience.

I was to meet my therapist at 8 o'clock the following morning down in the mysterious basement of the hotel where mere tourists were not allowed. Stepping out of the lift was time-travelling back to the 50s with mosaic tiled walls and notices in chunky writing pointing to *APPLICAZIONI DI FANGO.* Peering through the steamy atmosphere, I could see corridors and cubicles, men and women shuffling about in towelling robes, and rows of coloured chairs with spiky chrome legs, where people were waiting for treatment.

An elderly woman in a white overall and white clogs appeared and demanded my prescription. She glanced at it, gestured at me, and I meekly followed my mud matron to a cubicle where I uncertainly stripped off whilst she barked out the order on the prescription.

"Do I take everything off?" I asked timidly.

"Everything, signora," she confirmed.

No sooner had I stripped off than a man appeared, wheeling

a truck bearing six buckets of steaming chocolate-coloured mud whilst I tried to hide my nakedness behind the door. My mud therapist tipped one bucket's contents onto a rubber sheet on the bed, spread it out with a large paddle and drew a line where I was to put my bottom. Gingerly, I lowered myself onto it. It was almost too hot to bear. Briskly, she told me to lie down, and began tipping the other five buckets over me, smoothing it out and covering every inch apart from my face. I couldn't move: it was heavy and indescribably hot. The only consolation was that it didn't smell. Finally, the ends of the rubber sheet were wrapped over the mud and I was completely encased.

"*Venti minuti,*" she said and left me to my slimy hot fate.

Panic began to set in. I could just about move my head, but couldn't see a clock anywhere. What would happen in 20 minutes? What if they forgot me? You'd have thought you could relax in the comforting soft heat, but the perspiration was rolling down my face into my eyes, and as my hands were trapped, I couldn't wipe it away. Very soon my eye sockets were full of sweat and I had to keep my eyes closed.

Mercifully, after what seemed like hours, the dragon in the white overall returned to mop my face.

"*Dieci minuti,*" she barked and trotted off again in her white clogs.

The next time she came in, my time was up. She began scraping off the mud until I was able to sit up, but slowly. Apparently lots of people faint at this point, I was informed with grim satisfaction. She pointed her paddle towards the corner where there were two vertical bars attached to the tiles. I was to hold them whilst she hosed me down. I decided at that point that if this was cold water, either I'd faint on the spot, or if not, pretend to, just to escape the torture. Thankfully I was sprayed with warm, not-too-powerful jets of water.

Once I was rid of the debris from the encasement by mud, I had to walk down the steps of my own personal plunge pool, a willing victim to being virtually scalded alive. Another *venti minuti* were to be spent sitting on the bottom step contemplating my navel whilst gently simmering and turning very pink in the cooking process.

A small room off my main cubicle contained a bed and lots of pristine white cotton sheets and towels. There I was to rest for – you guessed it – *venti minuti* . I had nothing else to do but listen to my stomach rumbling and wonder whether breakfast was still being served upstairs. I couldn't relax. My mind was racing with the idea of my narrow escape from being boiled alive, and my body was trying in vain to return to normal.

I do believe my mud matron next came in with a glimmer of a smile, presumably because I'd survived thus far. (Or maybe she knew of further tortures to come.) She allowed me to put on my robe and propelled me through the steam along the corridor to two doors with heavy seals around them. Flashing lights on the wall nearby indicated a temperature of 49 degrees centigrade.

"You next have to spend 10 minutes in La Grotta, signora," she announced, and ushered me through the doors into a room of such intense heat that it would have been cooler to enter a hot oven. There was a faint sulphurous smell, and as I glanced round uncertainly through the vapour, I could see that in the middle of the room there was a six foot high mound of rocks, from the centre of which was issuing this hot steam, rather like a miniature volcano. She motioned me to sit on the stone bench which ran round the edge of the room. I did so, but shot to my feet again. Did she want me to have burn marks across my rear end? I made a pad of my dressing gown and gingerly sat down again. She waved goodbye with an airy

"Dieci minuti, signora,"

and shut the door. Adjusting to the scorching heat, I looked around the room. The walls were covered with tiny mosaics which had faded from a pale blue to a peeling cream, where they hadn't fallen off altogether. The ceiling was covered with large water droplets which every now and again dropped down to the floor or onto me. It didn't matter. In two minutes I was absolutely soaked in sweat. I was having difficulty breathing, and tried gently drawing the air in through my mouth because my nose couldn't take it. Gulping the scalding air didn't help, so I tried again to breathe slowly through my nose and began to master the technique. I was the only person in La Grotta, so there was no one to answer my questions or give me reassurance.

I later discovered that this was the only surviving authentic natural source of hot steam in the area and the *albergo* had been deliberately built right over the top of it. There are other caves in the hills with similar sources of very hot steam, but they've rightly been bricked up as dangerous.

After what seemed like an age, but was probably only five minutes, I'd had enough. This time, I wasn't imprisoned by a shroud of heavy mud and could move about. The door wasn't locked! I escaped. Outside the sealed door there was a row of seats where I parked myself until I was collected like a naughty school girl for the next phase of my treatment. I hung my head in shame at her tut-tutting for coming out before my time, and meekly followed Madame Mud.

We made our way down the corridor through a double door marked *MASSAGI.*

Another door marked *INALAZIONI* was half open. I could see through it a row of buttons and flashing lights rather like the flight deck on an aeroplane. Several people were sitting in a line programming the output of steam from funnels opposite their faces. Large notices above the inhalers reminded clients not to smoke. This could only be Italy.

I waited, with a few dated and well thumbed Italian celebrity magazines for company, until the masseuse was free. I noticed that there were two doors, and one was for a masseur. I hoped and prayed that I'd get the woman, not the man. He looked very tough, and I imagined he wouldn't be very gentle with me, and I'd become increasingly delicate as the morning had gone on. My prayer was granted. The woman beckoned me in and I climbed onto the bed.

This part was bliss. Every toe and finger, every notch of my spine received individual attention. The massage oil smelt wonderful, and her strong hands pushed and pulled rhythmically whilst I fell into a trance.

Putting my robe, knickers and watch back on, I saw that it was almost ten o'clock. I charged back upstairs with my heart racing, feeling very much less fit than I had done a couple of hours earlier. I just managed to grab breakfast before they closed the dining room.

I asked myself as I sipped my caffe latte, if I felt any different. Phil said I looked like a boiled lobster. Perhaps I felt more supple than usual (though that was thanks, I supposed, to the massage, not the mud) but certainly I felt exhausted and light-headed rather than relaxed and pampered.

And did I continue with my prescribed four days of treatment at six buckets a day? After day two, I suddenly found we had an urgent appointment in Venice which involved catching the early morning train.

Taking a holiday in a traditional Italian spa town is always a fantastic experience. The art and architecture are wonderful, the food fabulous and the grown-up atmosphere very civilised. (It's always a boost to the morale to realise that you will usually be the youngest person there.) But don't take the entire package. Unless you have the constitution of an ox, my advice is, leave the hot mud to the Italians.

3. SIGNING THE ANTI-MAFIA DOCUMENT: bewildering aspects of owning property in italy

My decision to buy a flat in Montebello was made just three summers ago when the Venice train stopped at the little station, and we'd just enjoyed a perfect day. I said to Phil, sighing contentedly, that if I ever had the opportunity to buy a little place of my own in Italy, it would be right there.

At that moment, as fate would have it, I spotted a handwritten *VENDESI* sign on a large piece of cardboard stuck to a balcony on the second floor. Walking to the gate of the small building, I thought how convenient it would be: no need ever to hire a car to get there, shops, restaurants, ice creams and a castle within easy walking distance, and lovely vineyard-covered hills all around. But especially I was thinking about how it was just Italy for Italians, not a tourist trap, and I was glad I'd begun learning Italian. I noted the phone number and resolved to call when I got back to the *albergo*.

"Don't be stupid" said Phil. (And all those other things on the front page of this book.) But I was determined, and after rehearsing what I would say a few times, I wrote myself a script and tried the number.

The woman I spoke to sounded pleasant and spoke clearly, thank goodness. The price was € 114,000 which I thought I might manage, (the exchange rate was much better in 2007) so we arranged to meet the next day. No estate agent was involved, which meant we'd both save around 3%.

Maria was a bundle of energy showing me the apartment. She whizzed round demonstrating how to work the shutters and the canopy over the balcony, explaining why everything was almost brand new. (Her son, Antonio, had been a student at Padua University and had never bothered to cook in the three years he'd lived there. The oven was still wrapped in polythene, and there were live wires sticking out of the walls and ceilings waiting for lights to be fitted.) Then followed a patient explanation of how the agreed price would be manipulated.

In Italy there is an agreed price on property, on which tax must be paid (more on this problem later), and another agreed price for fixtures and fittings. (No tax.) Apparently most purchasers agree on an artificially low price for the property, and an artificially high price for the fixtures and fittings, thus avoiding as much tax as possible. In the end, by email, we agreed on an official purchase price of € 97,000 with the difference for fixtures, which included kitchen and bathroom fittings, air conditioning, a few items of furniture and a cherry wood bedroom floor. So far so good.

But to backtrack a little. I mentioned what I'd been doing to a fellow sunbather at the local swimming pool. She was horrified and said I must look at other properties to be satisfied that the flat was good value. It was good advice but it didn't change my mind. I saw three other apartments – all larger and cheaper than mine, but which all needed decorating and alterations. One had a summer and a winter kitchen. Another had a lovely little kitchen garden next to the garage, and a wine cellar in the basement. The largest had belonged to an old lady and came complete with her antique furniture and two Murano glass chandeliers at the bargain price of €105,000. I was tempted, but held fast. It was too gloomy, in a building full of very elderly people, and I wanted to feel carefree, not compelled to do DIY when in residence.

My first challenge was to obtain an identity number (*Codice Fiscale*) to confirm that I am an Italian tax payer. Luckily Maria and her son, pleased to have a buyer, helped me with this and made me an appointment in a neighbouring town to sort out all the paperwork.

Something about rubber stamps seems to appeal to Italians. Every office I enter has rows of them waiting to be banged down in triplicate on endless sheets of paper. Meanwhile, I'm always conscious of the growing queue behind me, but Italians seem resigned to it, and always wait patiently. It was the same with opening an Italian bank account.

"Don't go to a bank. They charge a fortune. Use the Post Office Bank."

I duly did, but how old-fashioned it all seems. They keep a box file of my account details, rather than storing data electronically, but at least they've sorted out automatic payments for my utility bills. And here is something else I hadn't bargained for. There are two rates for gas and electricity in Italy, the higher tariff being charged for second homes, which of course mine is.

The second challenge was more complex. It hinged on whether I could be categorised as *Residenza* or *Domicilio* for the purposes of buying property. Italians I knew argued heatedly about it. They claimed I should be *Residenza* because it was my first property in Italy (and therefore only a 3% tax to be paid) rather than the 10% *Domicilio* tax for a second home. The Consulate in Venice was very helpful, replying with a list of recommended English-speaking solicitors from which I chose one at random. He replied by e-mail in exemplary English, confirming, sadly, that I have to be classed as *Domicilio.* Amazingly, he didn't charge me for his advice.

Luck was on my side when it came to payment. In the past couple of years the pound has plummeted against the Euro and I'm pretty sure that I couldn't have afforded the flat at today's exchange rate. I investigated various ways of transferring the money. There were standard fees of around £25 and only average exchange rates from two banks, but then I tried one of the specialist firms which advertise in the pages of the weekend broadsheets. (Tor FX) My money was sent by CHAPS electronic transfer at a far better rate for no additional fee. It was a hairy few days whilst I waited for confirmation that the money had been received, but it all went smoothly.

In Italy both the vendor and the buyer use the same solicitor. (*Notaio*) People complain about Italian bureaucracy but this actually makes things a lot simpler. (I think probably what they're really complaining about is the amount of money that most *notaios* earn.)

At the end of October I accompanied Antonio to see our *notaio*. I'd been forewarned to answer "*sì*" to any questions, because otherwise I'd have to pay extra for an official translator. The office was luxurious: flowers, original paintings on the walls and bowls of sweets for clients. We were ushered in to meet a very courteous middle-aged man who enjoyed using his few words of English. Fortunately, because he spoke slowly and clearly, I actually did understand what was said, as he mainly read from copies of papers I had in front of me. Twenty minutes later, the apartment was mine, with the documents to follow in two months. My legal fees, expenses and taxes came to € 4,800.

Antonio's whole family took us out for a celebratory fantastic meal that evening. Would that happen in England? I think not. There was much clinking of glasses of *prosecco* and general vowing of a new friendship, which it has turned out to be.

If I need a handyman, or someone to mop the stairs when it's my turn and I won't be there, Maria helps me to sort it out with neighbours. And that goes for the whole village. When we bought a washing machine, I asked about an electrician to fix the wall lights – there weren't any, just wires coming out of holes in the walls. They got straight on the phone to Dario, and when he offered to come in a couple of days, they said no, he must go immediately because we had no lights. (Not true. We were managing perfectly well with reading lamps.) Dario duly turned up in 10 minutes and worked for 4 hours fixing everything, then came back the following morning for another hour to do a little re-plastering. And for all that work he asked forty euros.

Marta, who runs the haberdashery, gives me her home made pasta, farmers give me their wine and olive oil, we get free ice creams at the local pizzeria. In summer neighbours and friends give us their home grown tomatoes, aubergines and courgettes, and when they make cherry jam, we're always given a jar. I do things the locals do. I can find my way to the nearest IKEA, and I shop at Ratti, a treasure trove of hardware and *batterie de cuisine* in Venice. It's a real boost to morale to be greeted by name when shopping in Padua or Venice. I feel I belong.

My flat is in a block of eight, and we all take it in turns to sweep and mop the stairs once every eight weeks. This seems to work quite well. There's a list of names and dates in the entrance, and when I'm back home in England I have established an arrangement with my neighbour to do my turn, and I do his in exchange when I'm in residence. Then there's the general maintenance. There are gardens in front and at the back, and the block is surrounded by a hedge. Twice a year there are bills to be paid for lighting, and to the gardener. This seemed to be working quite well until recently when I detected a bit of unrest. By law every *condominio* must hold a meeting of its flat-owners at least once a year. I wasn't aware this had happened, but I did see a group in earnest discussion by the gate on my most recent visit. The tall dark man who puts up the notices beckoned me over.

"Signora," he said. "Do you wish to save money on our bills?"

Silly question. Of course I did, and I said so.

"Very well. In that case I'm sure you will agree that we should buy a lawn mower and electric hedge trimmer which will pay for themselves in a year."

Although by now I manage to get the drift of what's said to me, my vocabulary doesn't stretch to infrequently used words like hedge trimmers and lawn mowers. I indicated that I was happy with the way they organised things and went off to the garage, puzzled by the conversation. Later the same day, my neighbour Sergio rang the bell. Sergio is in about his late seventies and is becoming a little frail. He explained to me that he wasn't happy about the idea of each taking it in turn to do the gardening, as it was too much work for him. He said he assumed I wouldn't like the idea either because I'm not always there. Once I understood, I agreed with Sergio. I didn't see myself wielding a hedge trimmer, especially as there are several ball-shaped miniature trees in pots near the entrance, and I had visions of irreversibly changing their shape, or lopping them off entirely.

"Good," said Sergio. "That is three out of eight so far. The woman with the dog in flat three is on her own and doesn't want the extra work."

I'm now in a state of suspense before my next trip to see how it all works out.

After my first year at Montebello I realised that I hadn't yet paid my local taxes for rubbish and amenities. I began to worry about exactly how much the bill might be, and decided to go to the *Municipio* to find out. This wasn't as easy as it might sound. It's only open on certain days of the week, and then only between certain hours. Studying the notice board outside the *Municipio* didn't help much because I couldn't work out which office I needed to sort out my payments. After several aborted attempts when the *Municipio* was open but not the relevant office, I finally got to meet the man in charge of the rubbish tax, Davide. I explained why I had come. He began to laugh and took out a battered exercise book where he kept phone numbers. I sat there listening whilst he related with amusement that he had an Englishwoman opposite him who actually wanted to pay her taxes. When he finally put the phone down, grinning, he asked me if I'd received a bill.

"No," I said.

"Well, in that case, signora, you cannot pay."

This was beginning to sound promising, but all the same, I knew I'd have to pay some time, which is what I tried to explain. We then began a kind of plea bargaining procedure.

Recently the locals have been incensed to discover that the area of their living space is now calculated from the external perimeter. In other words, the area, and therefore the cost, has become larger, even though the space remains the same. We now all have to pay extra for the bricks making up the walls. But there was nothing I could do about it, so we discussed how much I needed to pay.

We had to agree how much time I spent each year in Montebello, and whether I was alone or with Phil, and whether other friends might stay there from time to time. The local tax is charged per square metre, plus rubbish charges to be paid, Davide and I agreed, for an estimated five months of the year when I expect the flat to be occupied.

"But what about last year?" I asked, still concerned about the total amount I owed and some large lump sum looming on the horizon.

"Well, signora, since you received no bill, you cannot pay. 2007-8 will be free. From now on you will receive a bill."

I couldn't believe my luck. I can't see this ever happening in a larger town, but here they seemed free to make up the rules as they went along. I imagine it saved an awful lot of form-filling and rubber stamping just to let me off. Davide and I shook hands on the deal.

"Now, signora. Do you have bins?"

Of course I did. How did he imagine I was dealing with our rubbish?

Davide was shocked.

"But did you actually buy them? Do you have the receipts? I will refund the cost."

I explained that I had expected to buy my own rubbish bins and had certainly not kept any receipts. Davide shook his head as if to indicate what an uncivilised place England must be if people have to pay for their own bins, but I was perfectly happy with the arrangements I'd made.

The collection of rubbish in Montebello is very complicated. *Umido*, waste food, is collected twice a week. During our first few weeks in residence I felt quite hurt to discover my small sad little bag of *umido* had been left behind when the others had been collected. Later, I found out that it has to be stored in a biodegradable bag. Then there's *plastica-lattine* (plastic and tins), *vetro* (glass), *carta* (paper and cardboard), *verde* (garden waste) and *secco* (everything else). Every day a different category is collected: you need the municipal calendar to check. It's all taken very early in the morning so you put it out the night before, in differently coloured bags provided by the *municipio*. (The only bag that isn't provided is for *umido*.) This year, unfortunately, we weren't here when they delivered the calendars. This put me in the humiliating position of sneaking out at night to poke around in other people's rubbish to see what they'd thrown out.

Another trip to the *Municipio* to collect a calendar was the only solution. I always allow about two hours for any visit there. As I said before, it's never obvious which office to go to, or even whether the particular office you need will be open. And I'd just read the results of a survey in the *Corriere della Sera* which found that the average time spent queuing in Italy each year was 10 hours 23 minutes. This time I was lucky. I was only passed to three other departments in three short queues, then I was rescued by Davide who handed over a new calendar from his stock pile and I came out waving it in triumph.

As well as my personal concession for the rubbish tax, I'm also the beneficiary of other less formal deals now that I have a residence in Montebello. When we moved in, I went down to our beloved *albergo* to explain to Signor Bianco that we wouldn't be *clienti* any longer.

"Signora," he said with a slight bow of the head, his customary courtesy when you have stayed in the *albergo* for six years. "You are always welcome to use the pool whenever you like."

I was delighted and said so. It was virtually as good as having bought a flat with a swimming pool. He smiled, kissed my hand, and said we were part of the *albergo's* family.

Finally, the wonderful *Municipio* has put Montebello on the map. Yes, our little village has made national news: people in the *Bar Centrale* were interviewed for television, and the *Corriere della Sera* carried an article about our local council. All the fun was about an advert for local wardens *(vigili)* who seem to be a combination of traffic wardens, community police and market superintendents. The appointments were to be made after a short test, and extra points would be awarded if candidates spoke Venetian dialect. This brought howls of protest from politically correct factions who believed it was discriminatory, but my friend Davide at the *Municipio* justified it with a shrug of the shoulders.

"Most of our old folk only speak dialect," he explained. "We don't want them to feel left out."

I'm trying to imagine an equivalent appointment in Newcastle specifying that candidates should have a broad Geordie accent. All those self righteous clerks in the Personnel Department (who now call it Human Resources, as if we are mere commodities) would never let such an advert past their right-on scrutiny.

And what about signing the anti-mafia document? When the *Municipio* finally sorted everything out I was asked to sign this ominous-sounding piece of paper. No one as yet has given me a satisfactory explanation as to what it is. Italians, I have discovered, have an allergy to saying they don't know. I've heard many tentative explanations about this document, but nothing convincing. All we agree is that the Mafia's a bad thing, and that we are all in principle against it.

4. IN SHELLEY'S FOOTSTEPS: life in the hills

Our friend from the *albergo*, the Man With No Voice, announced one day that we were going on an expedition to the neighbouring town of Este. This was a few summers ago when he'd arrived with a glamorous mistress who wasn't, for once, an ice cream addict, so there was no need to go up into the hills in search of a *gelateria*.

Este is a pleasant little town with lovely municipal gardens laid out inside the castle walls, and a large cobbled square bordered with shops and cafes. We casually mentioned, not wanting to sound too learned in front of our companions, that Shelley and Byron lived in Este for a while, according to our guide book.

"Whereabouts?" was the response. "We'll go and see."

The book said they had stayed in Villa i Cappuccini which Byron had rented for two years. In fact Shelley had written two of his most famous poems in the summer house at the end of the garden. The Man With No Voice began accosting people to find out in his rather intimidating way (speaking in a husky croak rather like Marlon Brando in *The Godfather*) where exactly this villa was.

It turned out to be on a lane behind the castle walls, and it was obviously being renovated. The entrance had heaps of sand and cement around the gates, and the villa itself was encased in scaffolding. DANGER KEEP OUT signs were everywhere, and we turned to leave. Not so our leader. He moved a wheelbarrow out of the way, and stepped over a chain on which was suspended a sign which read PRIVATE PROPERTY.

"Follow me," he croaked, beckoning with his arm, and disappeared through the trees. We hung back. We could hear him tramping through the undergrowth, trying to find someone to talk to. He came back for us and chivvied us forward towards the villa. According to him, we were important English visitors, experts on poetry who had travelled expressly to see the villa and could not be turned away.

The workmen stood aside courteously, ushering us on to private property as if we were the owners. There wasn't much to see. The rooms were empty and dark, with shutters closed. However, we soaked up the atmosphere and imagined the poetic inspiration which went on here.

It left an impression, though, sowing the seed of an interest in these romantic poets who came to "our" hills. When we next went to Rome, we visited the graves in the lovely Protestant Cemetery, and the Keats and Shelley house at the Spanish Steps, something we'd known about but never bothered to see. It was morbidly fascinating, with the room where Keats died, and his death mask; and letters, etchings and books of everything remotely relevant to their lives. I bought a copy of Shelley's poems there, since it contained his *Lines Written on the Euganean Hills* and decided to find out more. The poem isn't particularly exciting, but it does contain one or two memorable lines and phrases:

> All is bright and clear and still
> Round the solitary hill.
> Beneath is spread like a green sea
> The waveless plain of Lombardy.

Shelley hadn't quite got his facts right. Solitary hill? There are 17 extinct volcanic cones here. His geography wasn't too hot either. The great plain you can see from vantage points on the hills isn't Lombardy but the Veneto, either towards the Venetian Lagoon, or westwards towards Vicenza.

In one direction you can clearly see the most southerly volcanic cone of Monselice. It's a charming small walled town with a grand castle and a lovely *palazzo*, but also has, according to my detailed guidebook, a small early villa designed by Palladio. We decided to investigate, assuming a building of such importance would be signposted, but no. This is villa country, where aristocrats built their grand mansions in renaissance times, and Palladian villas are almost ten a penny, as Signor Gondola (for that was his real name) came from nearby Vicenza. It was agreeable wandering round the town, but as there was no sign of a Palladian villa, we decided to ask in the local *tabacchi*.

"Could you tell us where Palladio's villa is, please?" we asked the friendly shop assistant.

"*Certo, signori.* What is his full name?

Somewhat puzzled, we gave the information. "Andrea Palladio."

The tobacconist disappeared into the back of the shop and re-emerged after a few minutes shaking his head.

"Sorry, *signori.* I've looked up Andrea Palladio in the telephone directory and he doesn't live here."

Looking further to the east, you see the view that Shelley

most enjoyed. He muses on the Venice he can see in the distance, which even then was having problems with tourism, it appears. I like his dismissive phrase *the polluting masses*, which seems even more apt today, when the cruise boats come in, depositing thousands of people and their detritus every day with no benefit to the local economy. Venetians deeply resent the cruise ships, and I agree with them. (Why would they eat in local restaurants when all their meals are paid for on board? Why would they use local transport when they disembark right in the centre of the city?). Shelley refers to Venice as *a peopled labyrinth,* a perfect description of the bewildering layout of tiny passages where you lose all sense of direction.

His description of the vineyards in autumn exactly chimes with my own experience the first time I saw the landscape in October, which is when the poem was written.

> The red and golden vines,
> Piercing with their trellised lines

is an understatement when you witness the reality of the wonderful multi-coloured striped vineyards. Each variety of grape produces a different colour of leaf, and usually the varieties are planted in rows of two or three, marching up the gentle slopes in a gaudy Bridget Riley canvas of golds, vermilions and browns.

The *vendemmia* or grape harvest takes place just before the leaves turn to their autumnal best. A friend who works in the Montebello *tabacchi* invited me to go with him one Sunday morning in mid-September to help in the vineyards. Of course I said yes. What better way to become a part of village life?

We set off along a small lane and pulled in between two ancient gnarled olive trees. Enzo, the farmer, came chugging along in his *Ape* to meet us.

(If you haven't yet encountered these little multi-purpose small vans, you need to picture a hybrid of a little Fiat 500 with an open truck stuck on the back, a sort of motorised wheelbarrow. *Ape* means bee, which is of course the sound they make as they buzz along. I like the fact that *vespa* means wasp, so scooters too whizz by with a sting in the tail.)

The *Ape* was loaded with empty plastic crates, and a row of secateurs, one for each of us. Enzo drove down the space between the first two rows of vines dropping off crates at regular intervals. It's as if the vines had been planted with the little truck in mind: maybe they were. Any closer together and you wouldn't get a vehicle down there at all.

Enzo is a child of nature. In summer he lives in a ramshackle tree house which he built himself, surrounded by his hens, goats, horses and rabbits. The children of Montebello often come to see his animals and ride the horses. He has the brown weathered skin and unkempt hair of someone who spends every waking moment outdoors, and would look a bit wild and scary were it not for his kindly crinkled eyes. His philosophy is to live off the land as completely as possible, and in harmony with it. When he needs ready cash, he does a few jobs, then returns to his simple existence.

He handed me a pair of secateurs, explained what I was to do, (simple: just cut off the bunches and drop them in the nearest crate) and suggested we worked together, him on one side of the vines and me on the other. As we went along the row, he talked a good deal about vine growing and I felt rather privileged to be a part of this rustic scene. Of course whether I'd feel the same if I had to do it all day every day for several weeks is another matter.

We began to encounter bunches where the bottom grapes had been nibbled away. This was apparently the work of wild boars which come down at night tempted by Enzo's merlot grapes. I was surprised to find that these grapes were deliciously sweet: for some reason I'd supposed that wine grapes were rather sour. No wonder the wild boars enjoyed them so much. Enzo seemed particularly pleased that the *cinghiali* who invade his vineyards are very well fed. He claimed grapes gave the meat a better flavour. The bare stalks they left had to be cut off, and the rest of the bunch dropped into the crate.

I was reminded of a headline in the local newspaper earlier in summer. Apparently some animal rights activists had released ten wild boar piglets which had been given a start in captivity on a local farm. All the people of Montebello were up in arms about the stupidity of these campaigners, saying the little boars wouldn't last two minutes in the hills. I'm sure they were right. Every weekend I watch from the balcony as vans and *api* head for the hills loaded with guns and dogs. In every lay-by you'll see a hunter's van parked next to a sign which reads *divieto di caccia* (hunting forbidden). Italians love hunting, and the released young wild boars had become fair game. At least as adults they might have had a sporting chance.

Now and then we came across little nests in the vines. Enzo told me the names of the birds, but my Italian isn't sophisticated enough to contain a vocabulary of bird species, and you tend not to carry dictionaries when you're harvesting grapes. Sometimes the nests contained a single unhatched egg, a tiny porcelain jewel, but Enzo explained that they were probably from the second brood.

As we worked our way along the rows, cyclists would whizz by up the lane, and shout greetings to us. Cycling provides Italian men with yet another opportunity to dress up. (Other than wearing tights in mediaeval pageants.) Each group of cyclists wears the identical brightly coloured spandex all-in-one suits of their club, complete with matching helmets. They seem to hold conversations even at high speed, and I've come to recognise the characteristic rush of air and noise as they flash by.

After about two and a half hours it was time for a break. We loaded the crates onto the A*pe* and followed it along the lane to the farmhouse where the huge wooden vats and wine presses had pride of place in the outbuildings, and the air was so heavy with the scent of fermenting grapes that mere breathing could make you feel drunk. And on all the lanes round about, tractors were chugging slowly along with their precious cargo of grapes gently being negotiated over pot holes. (They must be transported gently: the flavour will be spoiled if the fruit gets knocked about.)

Everyone traditionally drinks *mosto* for refreshment. This is the freshly squeezed juice, perhaps at most two or three days old, and utterly delicious. We all sat along a trestle table in the courtyard chatting, drinking the juice and eating slices of sausage with crusty bread. I was paid for my morning's work in bottles of red wine, and was eagerly anticipating a leisurely late afternoon resuming work on the next few rows, but no.

"We're off to the Festival of Grapes now," declared Enzo. "Put all the secateurs and boxes back in the barn."

We piled into an assortment of scruffy agricultural vehicles including the *Ape,* with children and the dog in the open truck, and set off in procession for the nearby village of Lotto. The car park was, appropriately enough, in a vineyard, between the rows of vines. Along Lotto's main street were the usual stalls selling balloons, toffee-covered nuts, and more things than you could ever imagine made from olive wood.

Loud, slightly military music was emerging from loudspeakers attached to lamp posts, and self-important marshals wearing fluorescent lime green waistcoats brandished table tennis bats to keep the crowds at bay.

Suddenly the marching music stopped and an incomprehensible announcement was made, followed by much cheering. The decorated floats were on their way.

I found myself shuffling back against the wall as a marshal, vigorously waving his paddle, indicated that the first float needed a lot of space. Who should I find there next to me but Maria from Montebello, so I managed to get a full explanation of what was happening.

"Every village in the hills makes its own float, entirely from grapes," she explained. "Competition is very fierce. Last year people complained about the waste when individual grapes were stuck into the wire templates, so this year the images are made using bunches which can be eaten afterwards."

Round the corner came a massive claw holding several kilos

of grapes. It was attached to a giant fox, and moved to and from the fox's mouth as it fed. Each time the claw came towards us, we shrank against the walls so as not to be gathered up and eaten, and so did the spectators on the other side of the street. Little children half cried in that delicious state between fear and fun, and we all clapped as the proud wine producers of Attesto chugged by with their fox.

I've no idea why the residents of Baone had chosen an Egyptian theme, but we next saw a huge pyramid covered in grapes being pulled along by a tractor. Every so often the top lifted and a cloud of smoke billowed out. Around the base were lots of nubile Egyptians with black hair and heavy eye makeup, waving to the crowds and throwing grapes about.

But nothing, not the grape castles, not the aquarium of grapes, even came close to the creation of the village of Teolo. We knew it was going to be good before it came into view because of all the "Bravos!" we could hear. Towering above us, higher than the tallest building, was a perfect replica of Michelangelo's David, made entirely from grapes. At times he shuddered when the tractor pulling him stopped momentarily, but he proudly stood in all his naked glory, perfect in every detail apart from a certain greenness not to be seen in the original. Shelley would have been inspired.

Judging was unnecessary. We cheered as he glided uncertainly by, twice round the village square before being torn to pieces and eaten.

The serious feasting then began. Several wooden huts had been erected in the square, each one advertising the wines of a local producer. You bought a book of vouchers for five euros and then exchanged them for glasses of red, white and sparkling wines, and cheeses and sausages with freshly baked bread. (They'd even set up portable bread ovens in the square.) A local band played traditional music, and we danced the night away *sotto le stelle.*

* * *

The city of Padua is our regional capital, and produces a free booklet every month called *Padova Today*. Whenever I'm in Padua I pick up a copy to see what's on, and diligently try to support local events like the many festivals - of peas, cherries, frogs (a communal feast with frog risotto followed by deep fried frogs' legs), or most bizzarely, knitting (the leaflet shows a photo of half a dozen matrons in a row on stage knitting furiously whilst a straggle of onlookers with presumably little else to do watches them); the music concerts in the grounds of Palladian villas; and the canal pageant. I have a suspicion that Italian men rather like wearing tights, (a theory I expand on in a later chapter) even in hot weather: there are so many mediaeval fairs with processions in costume and lots of flag waving.

In the May edition of *Padova Today*, an announcement about a literary event involving Shelley caught my eye. It appeared to be a lecture on his poetry and we felt duty bound to lend our support. The venue was a villa at Galzignano Terme. We parked there and went into the local *tabacchi*, the obvious place to ask about what's going on. The small group of customers had never heard of the villa and denied its existence in Galzignano. But it gave them something to do on a quiet morning, so word spread until someone was found who knew the answer.

An old man told us we needed to drive up the mountain

road round four hairpin bends until we came to a cross roads. The villa was along the lane on the right. We almost turned back at that point because we realised we were going to be late, but curiosity drove us on.

After many twists and turns we arrived at a large farmhouse with a modern glass annex which proclaimed itself to be the very villa we were looking for, a mountain refuge and information centre for the regional park. It was hard to find anywhere to park as the car park was overflowing and the whole site was on a steep slope, but in the end we tucked the car into a small space and walked up to the villa. Lots of hikers were standing outside, but the rooms where we'd expected to find an attentive audience were empty. Perhaps no one was interested in the poems of Shelley. I asked one of the outdoor types who seemed to be in charge of a group where the lecture was, showing him the entry in *Padova Today*.

"Oh no, signora," he laughed. "There is no lecture. We are walking to the spot on the top of Monte Venda where Shelley wrote his poem, and there we will read the work in translation."

Wow! Imagine say forty English walkers setting off on a climb to read Dante. Not a chance.

We were invited to join them, and would have done so except that we were only wearing light sandals and were totally unprepared for a climb in the midday heat. Once we'd seen off the literary hikers and watched them slowly climbing the path through the chestnut trees out of sight, we realised it was lunch time.

A meal with a view would be good, and as we were already more than half way up Monte Venda, the highest volcanic cone of the Euganean Hills, we thought we might try an *agriturismo* recommended to us by a friend in Padua. (Often the best places to eat come by word of mouth and are not to be found in the information dished out at tourist offices.)

The hamlet of Faedo is at the end of a short gravel track through vineyards, just a church, a cluster of houses and a farmhouse, now offering meals at weekends and bed and breakfast to hikers. Everything they serve is grown or raised on the premises: the place is surrounded by orchards, vineyards, olive groves, bee hives, a kitchen garden, and areas for poultry. (Their quail are particularly good.)

But best of all is the view from the terrace in front of the farm house. The simple wooden tables are grouped under an awning of bamboo canes, with pots of red geraniums at intervals along the balustrade. The land slopes away quite steeply, facing a series of wooded volcanic cones in a semi-circle, the space in between often filled with buzzards hanging in the hot still air. Between the cones, the flat hazy landscape of the North Italian Plain melts into the distance.

It was hard to find anywhere in Faedo to park when we arrived. In fact, we almost turned back, believing that they must be fully booked for lunch. However, as we were soon to discover, it was because there was a wedding in the little church.

As we sat waiting for our *antipasti*, the bells began to ring out and the church doors were flung open. (All this we could see from our table on the terrace. The church is across a small square to the right of the *agriturismo*.) The guests flocked out to prepare to throw rice over the happy couple. Then a tractor drew up outside the entrance. It was pulling a trailer covered with a white sheet on which were tied two dining chairs decorated with flowers, and a wonky yellow parasol had been fastened to the chairs at a jaunty angle. After much noisy laughter, the couple climbed aboard and were pulled, looking rather precarious, down the hill, followed by a long procession of all the wedding guests tooting their horns. From time to time we saw the procession below us as the narrow road reached a clearing on a bend, but we heard the joyful noises long after the line of cars disappeared entirely from view.

I don't know what Shelley would have made of the wedding party, or whether those intrepid hikers on top of Monte Venda could see it far below as they read his poem, but we revelled in the happy atmosphere and tucked into a long leisurely lunch. It was here that we encountered deep fried zucchini flowers. A huge mound of them, piping hot, was delivered to our table to accompany their home produced *prosecco*. Each crisp, melt-in-the-mouth morsel disappeared so quickly that our waitress asked if we wanted more. Silly question. Of course we did. The antipasto was repeated: we could have continued with the fried flowers and abandoned the rest of the meal, but it would have been a shame not to have sampled the roast quail…..

* * *

The *Padova Today* leaflet was responsible for another misunderstanding. I read that there was to be an outdoor concert in Vo, so we set off around the hills in good time. Of course when we reached Vo no one knew what we were talking about. I finally found an old man who suggested it might be on the road to Castelnuovo (great to discover there's another Newcastle in the area) but it was siesta time there and the whole village was fast asleep. Eventually I came across a cyclist dozing under a tree. He suggested I knocked on someone's door, which I was very reluctant to do. Slowly he stretched and got to his feet. He was a giant of a man, making a very imposing figure as he strode to the middle of the road in his clinging lycra and put his hand out to stop the next car. Amazingly, the driver knew where the concert was, so we set off again back down the hill armed with good directions.

There were lots of cars near a *strada bianca* (unsurfaced road) and we set off to walk up the hillside into the woods, not quite believing it was the right way until we heard applause coming from somewhere above us. We stepped into a clearing and there was a semi circle of rows of benches and people listening attentively to a harpsichord (how did that get there?) and flute. It was magical: music from Shelley's day performed in a local beauty spot he must have known. We'd missed half the performance by this time, but it was still utterly memorable.

* * *

In the great city of Bologna, hidden away in a tiny piazza behind the church of San Petronio, is a statue of Galvani, an 18th century physicist. What, you might wonder, has this scientist got to do with Shelley?

Look closely at the statue and you will observe that he is holding a tray onto which is pinned a dead frog. Galvani had discovered that a spark of electricity attached to the muscle of a dead frog made it jerk back to life. In doing so he introduced a new verb to the English language; to galvanise, to spring into action.

Curiously, Mary Shelley took his scientific treatise explaining about twitching frogs' legs as holiday reading when she travelled through Italy and Switzerland with Percy Bysshe and John Keats. I have no idea whether they collected any frogs for experimentation on their stay in the Euganean Hills, although frogs and toads are there in abundance. In fact, on a couple of roads there are warning signs to drive carefully during the breeding season for fear of squashing them, and there are also two local frog festivals each year in the hills, where frog risotto followed by deep fried frogs' legs and polenta are on the menu for the communal feast.

What we can readily surmise, however, is that this idea of reawakening from the dead insinuated itself deep into her unconscious thoughts, and Mary Shelley eventually came to write Frankenstein, one of the most famous Gothic novels ever written. I like to think that only now are the Euganean Hills being given due credit for this masterpiece of horror. Then again, perhaps my hills had nothing to do with it.

5.   LADDIE DEE AND OTHER MYSTERIES OF VILLAGE LIFE

I suppose you could say, if you like business-speak, that Federico the librarian facilitates my integration into the life of Montebello.

Our first meeting was when I decided to join the library, a modernist geometric building with a rectangle of glass bricks on one side, and a monument to the fallen of the two wars emblazoned on the other. Stupidly, I hadn't rehearsed what I would say as I approached the desk, but words came to me, even though they turned out to be hopelessly wrong.

"I'd like to add the library," I announced.

He looked at me kindly, but was obviously puzzled. I repeated my request, realising something wasn't quite right.

Producing an application form from a drawer, he very gently asked, "Is this what you want, signora?"

Gratefully, I took the form and ran away to avoid further embarrassment.

A couple of days later, I was back with the completed form and a dictionary in my handbag. No silly mistakes this time.

He glanced at the form and then looked at me over the top of his glasses.

"Pleased to meet you, Signora Robinson."

The only other person in the library, a rustic type who was probably having a rest from tending his vines, overheard our little exchange and began to whistle the *Here's to You, Mrs Robinson* tune by Simon and Garfunkel.

I'm used to this, of course. I always try to feign surprise and congratulate people on their wit, but actually it gets very tedious. However, I realised that this was an unusual moment in the history of Montebello's library, so we shook hands all round and I was shown the meagre selection of books in English. It was a curious collection consisting mainly of several Agatha Christies, a few books on horticulture and several biographies of explorers. I took a Henry James novel with useful footnotes in Italian, and asked when it was due back, as he hadn't stamped a date inside the front cover.

"It doesn't matter, *signora*. I know where you live. Keep it as long as you like."

The choice wasn't very promising, but I get through a lot of books down by the bubbling pool in summer, especially during siesta time when there's nobody to talk to or eavesdrop upon.

On my next library visit Federico took my elbow and escorted me to the far corner of the ground floor.

"*Ecco, signora,*" he said proudly. "I have moved all the English language books together onto this shelf. This is *your* shelf."

I now had a complete set of Shakespeare, some volumes of poetry, a few biographies of obscure twentieth century politicians, and an interesting random selection of nineteenth century novels about fallen women; Mrs Gaskell's *Ruth*, and Theodore Dreiser's *Jennie Gerhardt,* for instance.

I spent a lot of time in Montebello library round about the time of the giant cloud of volcanic ash over Europe, using the computers to try to find a way home. Naturally, other users were interested in my plight and each wanted to be helpful, suggesting various improbable or impossible routes, which led to lengthy conversations and a much wider acquaintance with residents of Montebello, some of whom wanted to practise their English on me.

The result of all this was that I was invited to give a talk in the library one evening, mainly in English but answering questions in (bad) Italian for the benefit of the community. They especially wanted to know why, out of the whole of Italy, I had chosen to live in Montebello. I agreed, and turned up at the allotted hour to be greeted by a recording of *God Save the Queen*, for which everyone stood up. The Councillor responsible for culture introduced me, saying she just had "*due parole*" to say. (Two words.) Half an hour later, I finally got to my feet.

I think lectures in the local library are usually quite formal affairs. I was determined this would be fun. I was armed with a large packet of *Jelly Babies* which I distributed for good questions or comments. Around thirty people had turned up, and it was all very jolly, adjourning to the bar until well after midnight.

Federico the librarian always alerts me to the various festivals that punctuate a year in the life of Montebello. They're very good at celebrating, and they love feasting and dressing up.

On Republic Day, veterans meet at the flagpole on the bridge over the canal, wearing their medals and *Alpini* hats, and carrying flags and wreaths. A white van, which is normally used to deliver washing machines, blasts out a continuous tinny recording of the Italian national anthem from two loud speakers on its roof, then follows us as we walk in procession to the next flagpole where another flag is hoisted to music and salutes.

This year the village celebrated the 800th anniversary of the building of the canal, and Federico wrote the script of the historic pageant to be re-enacted in the park one Saturday evening. Naturally we went along to show willing.

There's something a bit odd about Italian men's love of dressing up. They find any excuse to have a mediaeval procession in costume with lots of flag-throwing and drum-beating. What I can't understand is how they can bear to wear tights on a hot summer's day. I'm always glad to relinquish mine at the first sign of spring, and would have to be offered a very tempting sum to wear them again before October. But all the handsome young men of Montebello, far from thinking such things "uncool" happily exchange their jeans for tights at the drop of a plumed hat.

Nobody had warned us, as we took our plastic chairs in front of the improvised stage, that it wouldn't be a performance, more of a recitation, with people in turn coming forward in costume to read from a lectern. What was worse, the entire thing was in Venetian dialect and we understood not a single word. Thoughts quickly wandered onto subjects like were there any mosquitoes, what was for dinner, and how long to go. The fact that the local water company, sponsors of the event, gave everyone in the audience a free glass jug, was little consolation for an incomprehensible evening, but we did our bit, congratulating the participants.

One actor, who played the part of a 17th century merchant, in tights of course, works in a small printing press in Montebello. I had met him several times in the library, and was introduced to his wife in the little supermarket. Roberta never stops talking, with no concessions made for a foreign audience. On only the second time we met, she not only told me about her new teeth, but insisted on my inspecting and admiring them. She adopted us as trophies and invited us round for dinner one evening.

The Battistis live in a courtyard with an arched entrance which must at one time have been used for horses and carts. Four families live here, one on each side on the square, and on warm summer evenings they eat communally at a long table down the centre of the courtyard.

Instantly on arrival we became part of this noisy extended family, *proseccos* and introductions all round, and home made basic hearty fare: mixed salamis and prosciutto, a beautiful enormous lasagne, and roast chicken followed by mountains of fruit. It was like being in an opera set. Every so often someone would disappear indoors then stick a head out of an upstairs window to ask who wanted a second helping, or a plate of salad. Did I say ask? I meant, of course, shout, at the top of their voices, above the din below.

Roberta was curious about us. She pumped me for information and discovered that I'm a magistrate. At this important piece of news, she passed me her *telefonino* to ring her neighbours in the next courtyard. This unfortunate couple have a dog called *Menta* (Mint) which howls a lot, though how they ever hear it with the noise they make I can't quite understand. She wanted me to command them with the mighty authority of Her Majesty's Magistrates' Courts Service to quieten their dog. I tried to explain that magistrates in England are only voluntary and in any case I couldn't enforce an order in Italy, but she didn't believe me and was so disappointed when I handed the *telefonino* back again that she didn't speak for at least five minutes.

All was forgiven when I complimented her on her pasta; then I admitted I'd never made any. This came as a great shock to all females present, who asked if I could at least make gnocchi.

"Never tried."

Roberta clucked like a demented chicken and told me to report there tomorrow morning for a lesson. Not asked, just told. An offer I couldn't refuse.

Whilst we rolled our mashed potato into sausages on her floured oilcloth, I was grilled about a mysterious person called Laddie Dee. I denied all knowledge of this famous English person whom she insisted I must know. The penny dropped after a few minutes. She was talking about Princess Diana, "Lady Di". Even though she's been dead for a decade or more, Italian gossip magazines still feature her regularly with indignant comments about Charles and Camilla. Roberta and her cronies identify with these views and clearly didn't believe me when I tried to give a rather more balanced picture.

* * *

My car lives in Italy all summer. In winter we don't have a car there because we always drive it home for Christmas loaded with wines, *panettone* and other goodies. On our first winter stay, we were resolved that we should show our loyalty to the village and use a local car hire firm rather than the internationals like Avis, Hertz or whatever was available at the airport. I went into the library to ask Federico, and yes, he said, there was a hire firm on the outskirts of the village.

We tramped along one dreary damp morning to a large warehouse next to the cemetery. It seemed possible to hire anything but a car. There were cement mixers, diggers, tractors, and bizarrely, even traffic lights. Just think what gratifying chaos you could cause on a road by hiring a set of traffic lights. Anyway, we rather doubtfully asked the owner whether he had a car for hire. We were potential customers and he was clearly reluctant to say no. He said he'd have a car for us the next day if we came back at 10 o'clock.

We did. There was a car parked next to the warehouse, so we assumed it was ours.

"Oh, no. That's *my* car," said Rinaldo. "But I do have a minibus for you."

We looked at it with horror. It was a 15 seater with darkened windows and built like a coach with wing mirrors the size of doors on each side. The trouble was, we'd counted on having a car and had arranged to meet friends for a meal at a trattoria in the hills. Rinaldo could see our hesitation.

"You can have it for a bargain price," he offered. "Thirty euros a day all in, and bring it back whenever you like."

We reasoned that it was always quiet on the roads in the hills, even if they were on the narrow side with lots of hairpin bends. Perhaps it wouldn't be too difficult to drive a minibus there. After driving once round the cemetery to try out the gears and steering, we set off towards the hills.

The main railway line from Venice to Rome passes along the foothills, but they haven't yet got round to building all the tunnels and bridges they so badly need to cross the line. Joining a long queue at the level crossing, we switched off. It's generally a long wait because the line is very busy not only with Eurostars and local trains, but also with long goods trains and hundreds of new cars being transported south every day. Italians being the way they are, hate this delay in their journeys. They often risk having the crossing gates thudding down on their car roofs, so anxious are they to avoid a wait. Then of course, the minute the barriers begin to rise, they're off, responding as if to a starter's flag. This is an ideal spot for old codgers to congregate and watch what's going on. They often stand smoking in small groups a little beyond the level crossing: some even bring folding chairs. Whilst chatting away, they always go in for a lot of the scrotum adjustment that characterises Italian males in conversation.

The Eurostar hurtled through and the barriers began to rise. Cars jockeyed for position to speed ahead, and one coming towards us tried to overtake because the car in front wasn't off the mark quickly enough. Forgetting the width of the minibus, we swerved to avoid this maniac, only to knock over one of the old codgers with the gigantic wing mirror.

We screeched to a halt, nearly causing another *incidente.* (Typically, the Italian word for an accident is *incidente,* which somehow lessens the seriousness of what has happened.) Deeply troubled, we looked at each other. By mutual consent, and because my Italian is better than Phil's, I got out and walked back to where the old man was lying in the dust surrounded by his companions who were trying to help him to his feet. They glared at me and made all sorts of gesticulations which I took to be curses. I attempted in my feeble way to say how sorry I was, and played my trump card, the fact that we were English and unused to a left hand drive vehicle. Somehow, I don't know why, that seemed to make all the difference.

"Ah, *inglesi,*" they nodded, as if it explained everything. No doubt it would give them plenty to talk about over the next few weeks. The old man wasn't hurt, thank goodness, apart from the odd bruise. He actually kissed my hand as I left, as if to thank me for knocking him over.

After lunch, we took the minibus back to the depot and resolved to use buses or trains in future whenever we didn't have the car with us.

* * *

We spend a lot of time doing what the locals do, watching the world go by from the balcony. It's amazing what you learn about Italian life just by doing that. Take riding bicycles, for instance. Italians have a talent for riding bicycles with one hand. When it rains, they cycle along confidently under an umbrella, and of course in all weathers they chat away holding their *telefoninos* as they go. Alberto, the ancient handyman, regularly carries pipes, planks or even a ladder over his shoulder as he pedals down the road, and the ladies of a certain age cycle to church in winter in their fur coats. But nothing is as spectacular as the weekend performance by cycling clubs as they whizz by in a mass of brightly coloured lycra, the spandex ballet, chatting and waving, heading for a day's strenuous activity in the hills.

At around half past nine each morning we see a group of elderly gentlemen wearing their cycle clips and pedalling towards the fields on the outskirts of the village. We subsequently discovered where they are heading: to their "den" between the corn field and the vineyard next to the canal. The Euganean Hills are criss-crossed with lots of walks, all relatively without difficulty unless you want to climb, because they go round the various volcanic cones. One of those tracks, The Horseshoe Walk, cuts through fields and round the bottom of Monte Ferro, the nearest hill to Montebello. This is where the den is. Phil and I came across this ramshackle structure on a recent walk and wondered what on earth it was. First there's a wooden notice board with a little roof on it. These notice boards occur at regular intervals on the local walks, and usually have a map and an explanation of the flora and fauna to be found there. On this notice board there is no information. Instead it has been appropriated for use as a bicycle and umbrella stand, with plastic bags of useful things like balls of string and tools tucked under the roof. Next to the defunct tourist information is one of those wooden picnic tables which incorporates two benches. You can't actually see the table because it has been enclosed by plastic sheeting to make a little furnished room. We peeked inside. The occupiers have made it cosy with cushions, a primus stove and a rug or two. This little group of old cronies spends its time fishing in the canal and brewing coffee, well away from their wives and domestic duties.

But life is not always plain sailing for the cycling gang of oldies. The combination of old age, bicycles and Italian drivers is a recipe for the occasional *incidente* when one of their number is knocked over, causing much shouting and gesticulating, and drawing a large crowd. The latest was at the crossroads in the centre of Montebello, caused by a decorator's white van (*tinteggiatura e verniciatura)*. The victim was lovingly laid full length on a convenient bench, and his companions tended his wounds with the first aid sets they always seem to have to hand. He had plasters on his bald head, his hands and knees, and was lying with his eyes closed whilst half of Montebello waited anxiously for the ambulance, which arrived pretty promptly and noisily with its blue lights flashing. Having enjoyed all the attention, the injured old man opened his eyes and declared to the ambulance men that he was perfectly OK. He walked unaided into the ambulance to rousing cheers.

We can see and hear the main Venice-Bologna railway line from the balcony. That is the reason for the underpass which is directly opposite the building. Every so often a large lorry gets stuck in it, having taken no notice of the height warning signs nearby. We get a grandstand view of the resulting struggle to back out round the curve when the top is firmly wedged against the top of the *sotto passo*. This is a favourite piece of entertainment for the residents of Montebello. Luckily, the ice cream parlour is only round the corner, so the usual routine is to buy a *cono* and stand watching whilst they try to extricate the lorry without moving chunks of concrete at the same time. The *carabinieri* usually arrive on the scene and wave their paddles importantly at approaching cars, telling them to turn around and take a different route. There is always much shouting of advice, and a festive atmosphere which continues long after the offending *camion* has found a different route across the railway.

In late summer, the trees along the railway line attract early morning gatherers, picking the wild figs which grow there. They seem oblivious to the *Freccia Rossa* (red arrow) which hurtles by, inches away. The same goes for the snail collectors and the mushroom pickers. I've learned a lot about food for free just from my observations from the balcony.

Opening the bathroom side window, next to the balcony, the other day, I was astonished as I was brushing my teeth to see two young men, heads on a level with mine, slowly moving upwards in an open cage directly outside.

"*Buongiorno, signora,*" they chorused as if it were the most normal thing in the world to rise beyond the second floor like that. They were fitting a satellite dish on the roof. Before long, of course, a small crowd gathered to watch. The whole performance disturbed our neighbour Sergio who was busy as usual, making mysterious objects in the garden below. Sergio has become so important to our lives in Montebello that he deserves a whole section to himself. Read on, and all will be revealed.

6. THE DUCK WITH DETACHABLE BALLS: village characters

Unlike your average English towns, which are all the same nowadays, with a Boots, a Next, a W.H.Smith's…., Italian towns have individual character because most shops are still owned by families and are small and specialised, perhaps a shop which just sells gloves (there's a good one in Sorrento) or just hats (a tiny one in Venice, taller than it is wide).

It's the same with people. These days the English are losing their eccentricity. It must be something to do with everyone watching the same T.V. programmes, reading the same papers, indulging in the same habits, and being programmed to do so by the nanny state which tells us how to think and act.

Italians are different. It's interesting that the word the media use most often to describe Silvio Berlusconi is *spregiudicato* which is difficult to translate, but means unconventional and unscrupulous, someone who breaks the rules and doesn't care. You might think that it would be a pejorative description, but you'd be wrong: this is Italy. It's usually a compliment, especially when applied to the Prime Minister. He's regarded as a lovable rascal, a ladies' man. All Italian men of a certain age would like to be Signor Berlusconi.

Italians don't like to conform. This has its downside, especially when queuing, or paying taxes. How often have I felt infuriated when waiting in a shop or to buy tickets, having crafty *italiani* casually using the magic word "*permesso?*" as they sidle to the front of the queue. Then there've been countless occasions when we've been staying in a little *albergo* and given a discount if we paid cash. (No taxes payable, no questions asked.) Or the whole business of buying property and adjusting its value for tax purposes, as I described in chapter 3.

I've recently learned that in Naples, renowned in northern Italy for being a city full of cheats, the citizens have devised a special way of avoiding parking fines. As in many Italian towns and cities, Naples uses parking discs to display arrival times. However, this does not allow for the ingenuity of Neopolitans who have invented the clockwork parking disc. The arrival time simply moves on, alongside real time, so that the one hour limit never expires.

The result of all this lack of conformity is that every village is full of characters who are at once annoying, amusing, irritating, but never dull. Here are a few I've come to know well over the years.

* * *

Sergio, our neighbour, was once an engineer. Like many Italians of his generation, he is very good with his hands and can mend almost anything. Now in his late seventies, he sits outside his garage on a wooden stool (which he made himself, of course) hammering, soldering and painting all day long in the shade of his up-and-over garage door. Sometimes what he's doing is obvious. The locals often bring him bits of old bicycles they've found, and he puts them together to create hybrid models unified by a coat of silver paint. There are quite a lot of strange silver bicycles in our little town.

Now that I know him better, I often pass the time of day

on my way to the washing machine in our garage two doors down from his. I get enthusiastic descriptions of what he's currently working on.

What are you making today, Sergio?"

"Clocks, signora. When I am bored, I make another clock."

It was indeed the case. The whole garage was alive with ticking clocks of all shapes and colours, with hands made from scraps of metal he'd found lying around.

"Would you like one? I have made a blue one for you."

As a thank you I often give him items of rubbish which only he could find a use for. His eyes lit up at the prospect of a discarded umbrella, but he hasn't yet turned it into a clock.

Sergio is very skilful and imaginative with wood. As we were putting the car away one day we saw him erecting an interesting object on a pole in the garden. The pole itself was unusual: an iron rod twisted like barley sugar in true baroque style. On top of it was an exquisite wooden aeroplane varnished to a deep mahogany shade, with a whirling propeller. This was clearly special.

"Oh yes," said Sergio proudly. "It's for my grandson's garden."

Pity it won't be permanently on display near the row of garages.

But what was also occupying him was the creation of a hutch for his daughter's tortoise. Did I say hutch? I meant a luxury miniature bungalow, complete with windows, a round doorway and a hipped roof. Unfortunately when I asked Maria whether the tortoise had adapted to his new home, she snorted.

"Of course not. For a start he can't get his shell through the doorway. It's too small. And in any case, he doesn't want a varnished wooden floor. He likes to stand on the ground."

Other creations are more mysterious. He recently developed a craze for making odd creatures out of wire coat hangers. After a while, a strange menagerie began to appear around our block of flats. The first attempt was a dog, flat of body and with an odd tail, but recognisably a dog. The cockerel was rather more successful. Its beak was open in the act of crowing, and its tail feathers fanned out in a rainbow of colours. It was mounted on a revolving disc on a tall pole, with the later addition of a flat red arrow to make it into a weather vane. A helicopter followed, also on a pole, with wing and tail propellers twirling merrily. An interestingly shaped tree root was transformed into a sort of octopus, varnished and given glass eyes. A rather sinister edifice made of car wing mirrors appeared opposite our garage, but no one was spying on us. It was just another of Sergio's creations. Very soon the rose bed had been taken over by an army of curiosities on spikes.

My partner Phil became very interested in this development. He was struck by this naïve resemblance to the work of the American sculptor Calder, and decided to bring Sergio a book about Calder which he felt would further inspire him.

For a couple of days we didn't see Sergio, who had seized the book with great glee. Then he chased us down the street to show us the technical drawings he'd made based on Calder's images. He was fired with enthusiasm about making more and more, and thrilled to know that a famous sculptor had been showing pieces like his for years and making lots of money.

On our next return trip to Italy we found a note waiting for us in scarcely legible Italian. We were invited down to the garage to inspect the latest masterpieces. An elephant had now joined the collection, and a rather distorted cow with a massive udder. Best of all was a bundle wrapped up in an old oily cloth which he proudly presented to us as a gift. It contained a life-size wire duck complete with webbed feet on which it stood, a little precariously. But that wasn't all in terms of completeness. Sergio had made the duck a set of genitals, probably larger than in real life, which swung jauntily from a wire cross piece. He explained that he'd attached them to a magnet for reasons of modesty, so that we could have a less cocky duck, as it were, for visitors of a more sober frame of mind.

Delighted with the duck, we carried away our trophy to give it pride of place in the little flat. We occasionally have to remind ourselves and others:

"Remember, when his balls swing, the duck loses his balance."

* * *

You can virtually guarantee that whenever I open the shutters in the morning to observe life from the balcony, Alberto will be riding by on his bicycle, usually carrying his tool bag and assorted rods and pipes. Strictly speaking, Alberto shouldn't be riding a bike at all, with or without tools. He's 85, stocky and with only three teeth in his head (which of course doesn't hamper the bike-riding, but you get the picture). His face is permanently creased with good humour, and he's very bronzed from all his cycling. Throughout the summer he wears very short shorts, probably bought in the 60s, and a baseball cap which once was denim blue but is now so faded by the sun that its colour is indeterminate, like an English overcast sky.

Alberto is the village handyman. I was extremely doubtful about this when I first met him. It seemed a bit irresponsible to ask him to climb a step ladder to put up shelves at his age, and he didn't exactly look either strong or capable. However, he'd been recommended by the ever-helpful Maria, so I tentatively asked him whether he could hang a mirror for me. It took him a long time to measure the space and line things up, all of which did nothing to inspire confidence. Then he said that the hooks provided by Home Base (we'd brought the mirror from England in the car) were wrong, and he could get better ones. Off he went to the local hardware shop and returned half an hour later with perfect chrome hooks. I began to warm to him.

The next job was to put up four hooks and a shelf near the door. Alberto took out his ruler and pencil stub, and began making marks all over my pristine white wall. The maths seemed to be beyond him, dividing the short wall into four equal spaces. It wasn't just the increasing number of pencil marks that were worrying me; it was the fact that his hands were dirty and the wall was also filling with grubby hand prints. I politely suggested that he might like to wash his hands. He refused, saying with a grotesque smile something I didn't quite catch (remember he has only three teeth) about how it would be alright in the end. Of course it *was* alright in the end. He fixed everything perfectly then produced his master stroke. Instead of cleaning the wall as I'd expected, he took a screw driver and tapped away the marks with his hammer.

"*Ecco*, signora!" he said beaming, and indeed it was very good.

I saved the most taxing job until last. I'd bought a banner from a *palio* in Tuscany, and as it was exactly the colours of the bedroom, I wanted to hang it above the bed. I gave him a packet of small metal pegs with ring hooks attached, and asked him to fix a rod to the wall to hang my trophy.

I wondered if we needed to move the bed. No. I looked doubtfully at his shabby training shoes. Perhaps he'd like to take them off? No. (I later realised that he wasn't wearing any socks.) In the end I put some newspapers on the bed and we both climbed on board. In trying to hold the rod where I wanted it, we began to bounce and he began to laugh. Before long he was like a child on a trampoline, and he laughed until tears came to his eyes. He kept saying that he didn't have so much fun with his usual customers, and that the English were mad, but he managed to fix the rod eventually and hang up my banner.

Next came the question of his bill. I was left with a dilemma because I could hardly pay him the ten euros he asked. Unsure of the etiquette in such circumstances, I offered him twenty. He was delighted. Off he went on his bike, and I saw him ten minutes later cycling home with a new bicycle tyre over his shoulder.

I heard from our young neighbour, Nicola, that the youth of Montebello have rewritten a pop song to the tune of *Ghostbusters* in honour of Alberto. It goes something like (but in Italian)

> If there's something wrong
> In the neighbourhood
> If a shelf needs fixing
> He can saw some wood,
> Who you gonna call?
> ALBERTO!

Alberto loves this song and glows with pride whenever anyone sings it as he rides by.

We are now the best of friends. We meet him almost everyday, sometimes shopping ("Don't go to the Co-op, *signora*. Ali supermarket is better and cheaper.") and more often with jobs to do. First it's a hearty hand shake, oily dirty hands notwithstanding, then he produces impressive lists of jobs from his top pocket. Alberto says he'll always have time to come back to help the *inglesi*.

* * *

I once bought a fur coat in a charity shop years ago, when you could wear such things to keep warm without the fear of animal rights activists throwing a pot of paint over you. This fur coat has seen better days, and has been in a bag in the bottom of my wardrobe for the past decade, but I heard of a family of furriers near my village who could work wonders on moth-eaten bedraggled animal skins. And of course I'd be able to wear a fur coat in Italy without derision. Here, glamour counts far more than concern for the environment or animal welfare.

Via Bernini is a long narrow lane which winds through the vineyards along the base of the hills. Nobody uses this lane much, apart from the residents, because it doesn't really go anywhere.

We were looking for number 40, which didn't appear to exist. There was a woman tending her *orto* (kitchen garden) at number 42, so we asked her where her neighbours' house was, explaining helpfully that it was where fur coats were re-modelled. She gave us a strange look and denied all knowledge of the family, then rushed indoors.

A few yards down the lane there was an old iron gate which obviously hadn't been opened for about half a century. It was rusty and covered with creepers, and was held together with a padlock and chain which would probably have come apart if we'd put any pressure on it, but we thought we'd better not. Next to the gate was a gap in the wall where the old bricks had simply tumbled to the ground, possibly helped by one of those typical Italian drivers who in normal life is gentle, but once behind a wheel becomes a maniac who thinks he's driving a Ferrari, and whose car is covered with evidence of bumps and scrapes. We clambered over the bricks into a surprisingly well kept garden, with green grass (must use a sprinkler regularly) and pots of geraniums.

A large dog (or was it a wolf?) came hurtling towards us barking loudly and looking menacing. It was followed by a scrawny strange-looking woman, in a lime green boiler suit, hair in red rollers, and clothes in complete disarray, shouting and gesticulating wildly. She eventually grabbed the dog before it devoured us, and we nervously introduced ourselves as potential customers for the furriers. Yes, we were in the right place. She didn't seem at all surprised that we'd managed to find it. Maybe those in the know just take it for granted that you have to step through a breach in the wall and go to an unnumbered unadvertised house in the middle of nowhere.

(Actually, it all made sense later when I found out that of course this was yet another example of the favourite Italian pastime of evading taxes.)

The wild woman gripped my arm and pulled me along to the house, shouting at me all the time because I am foreign and therefore need to be spoken to at full volume. Every so often, she paused and looked at me, patted me appreciatively and said she'd show me all sorts of things, but not to tell anybody because it was a secret. This loud attempt to confide in me was accompanied by putting her finger to her lips. Clearly I was being admitted into a private world of some importance.

As we neared the house, I was shown a little area where she evidently spent time sunning herself. Aged around sixty, she had leathery skin and was as brown and wrinkly as a walnut. There was a strange contraption like a double rocking bed under an improvised awning made from old blankets. Around it were various small tables and cupboards stocked with magazines and glasses and a portable fridge full of bottles. With the usual Italian hospitality she invited me to join her there in her outdoor boudoir, but I declined.

She then dragged me off to the kitchen garden where her sister's husband was sitting on a stool sleeping with his straw hat pulled over his eyes. Just as well he was asleep: I gazed at him in fascination. He was the wartiest individual I'd ever seen. Warts covered every part of his face and body. He was like an old toad.

"Come on, signora," urged my companion. "You need some tomatoes and onions. Our melons are very good too." She threw several kilos of assorted produce into the back of our car, then led us to the house.

The Hound of the Baskervilles was pushed into a room near the entrance and we were ushered inside. Down a short flight of steps was a cool windowless area, off which were two large rooms. The first was filled with rails, lots of parallel rows which echoed the neat vineyards outside. Here were hundreds of fur coats spending the summer months in secluded chilly hibernation before their owners reclaimed them for the winter. Some had been cleaned and reconditioned, some were brand new.

I was pulled into the *laboratorio* next door. An older man and two youths were at work with piles of skins on large tables, scraping, stretching and cutting the pelts. The mad woman introduced me like some kind of trophy.

"Here is an Englishwoman!" she said triumphantly. They nodded shyly and got on with their work. She walked me up and down the room so that they could get a proper look at this strange exotic creature.

A beautiful marmot jacket caught my eye.

"Was that made here?" I asked.

It was. It had been made by the mad woman's daughter who now appeared on the scene and had a useful calming effect. My friend the mad woman stood back and watched. I tried the jacket on. How soft, how silky!

Reluctantly I unzipped the bag containing my humble charity shop coat. It looked like a drowned cat which had been nibbled by fish for a few months.

"Can you do anything with it?" I asked doubtfully.

Of course they could. She explained how it could be reconditioned and the bald bits disguised, all for the princely sum of 60 euros. ("But for you, signora, 50 euros") A bargain if they truly managed to do what they said. They knew, of course, that I had fallen for the marmot jacket. They could keep it for me until our next visit, I could pay in instalments, I could make a decision later, it would be twice the price in the fur shop in Padua…many options to tempt me. The clincher though was the mad woman's generous gesture. She scuttled off into another area and came back with a small bundle of fur.

"This is a present," she shouted, tapping her nose. "Don't tell anyone!"

It was a beautiful marmot muff. I have it with me now. I just need the jacket to match.

* * *

I used to be a bit scared of Bluto, before I knew his real

name, that is. When he patrolled the bubbling pools of mud at the little *albergo*, he seemed huge and menacing, chasing us away like naughty children. His face was Frankenstein-like, with a broken flattened nose and enormous forehead.

He used to sit a couple of tables away from us in the dining room. Other *clienti* always went up to him for a chat: he never budged. There seemed to be a lot of deference, and after a while, we found out why.

Chatting as usual in the pool, I managed to find a quiet moment when they weren't talking about food to ask who he was. They seemed very surprised that I didn't know.

"Why, signora, he's the ex-heavyweight champion boxer of Italy."

Not for nothing was he called Massimo. However, as a couple of years went by and we began to communicate in bad Italian, he must have decided that we were OK. We were admitted into his inner circle for little excursions in the evening. Luckily, The Man With No Voice was always there the week before, so there was no danger of offending anyone.

"*Tutto posto*, Pheel?" was his favourite greeting to us when we met in the dining room or at the pool. (He never attempted to pronounce *my* name.) Everything was of course always OK, and he approved of the fact that I enjoyed *prosecco*, using it as an excuse for our evening excursions to go to try the wines of yet another *cantina* in the hills. It was Massimo who first introduced me to *fragolino*, a mixture of *prosecco* and wild strawberries, sweet, refreshing and quite delicious.

One evening he announced that we were going to the nearby spa town of Abano where there was open air dancing *sotto le stelle* (under the stars). The convoy left as soon as the evening meal ended at about 9 o'clock. We all found plastic chairs to form a group near the space in the park where dancing had already begun.

Massimo led me onto the dance floor. As I only came up to his elbow, dancing with him felt rather odd. He seemed to like twirling me around under his arm and what with that and the *prosecco* I soon became dizzy. Massimo was enjoying himself, and I was enjoying the fact that he said it was like dancing with a feather because I was so small and light. I'm not either, particularly, but as he's so enormous, it made me feel dainty and delicate.

Dancing in a more sedate way with "Pheel" helped me to recover from the whirling performance, and we all watched the firework display before heading back to the *albergo*.

Massimo invited us to visit him at his home near Modena the following summer. He lives with his wife in a very large bungalow with nondescript views of the flat north Italian plain on every side. His wife, once a groupie I suppose, is rather like the ageing equivalent of an Essex girl – generous and pleasant, but a bit tarty. At the back of the house is one of those rectangular self-build swimming pools with sides of tough blue plastic supported by metal struts. To our surprise when we walked round the garden, who should be descending the step ladders from the pool but our old friend the *Presidente.* We all chatted over a coffee in the garden before going indoors.

The interior is Liberace style. There are thick shag carpets, candelabras, and lots of shiny surfaces covered with twee ornaments and photographs in ornate frames. Italians seem to like heavy pseudo-antique furniture, and Massimo and his wife are no exception. Display cabinets with leaded windows are filled with trophies and sentimental porcelain animals. The billiard room is different, though. Almost covering one entire wall is a blown up photo of our friend in the ring, fighting George Forman. I suppose, though I hardly liked to ask, that that must have been a successful fight, perhaps his best.

The improbable friendship now firmly established, we went on our way with promises to meet again, and the following year, Massimo duly arrived in Montebello for his usual week's mud treatment, but we weren't staying there any more, having by this time bought the little flat. We bumped into him in the village and explained that we now had an *apartamentino*, inviting him for an *aperitivo* that evening. He arrived with a large parcel, a present for his dear English friends.

When I opened it, I found an enormous pair of boxing gloves in bright red leather. They're now hanging from one of Alberto's hooks on the wall in the flat, a perfect reminder of one of our more unusual, and certainly the largest of our Italian friends.

7. THE GRAND DAME OF TUSCANY

It was dark, and the man in my life, who has no head for heights, was simmering on the point of eruption as we negotiated another hairpin bend on yet another Apennine mountain top in the middle of nowhere. There was a thunder storm, and it was pouring with rain. We were on our way from Montebello to stay in the guest cottage belonging to an amazing old woman we'd met who had invited us to stay at her place in Tuscany, where she owns a hill and all the buildings on it. At least when we found it, at the top of an almost washed away gravel farm track, the little Tuscan *casetta* had plenty of candles to see us through the power cut.

Flinging open the shutters the next morning, paradise! Brilliant light, with lavender-grey hills rolling gently into the distance, dotted with poplars, umbrella pines and vineyards. Our terrace, fringed with enormous terracotta urns, and alive with lizards, looked down on to an inviting pool sparkling in the sunshine. To the left, a tennis court, to the right, silvery green olive trees, an orderly vineyard, and a deer standing on the fringes of the woodland.

There was a note on the table in large spidery handwriting, along with wine and a basket of fruit, inviting us to a candle-lit dinner at the pool side to join our friend, the American owner of the property.

What a dame! In her 90s, she'd had four husbands, each one richer than the last, (which is presumably why she's been able to buy this little piece of paradise) and knew everyone who was anyone in Florence. Rather like an American version of Dame Edna but without the malice, she has bright blue bouffant hair, eyebrows drawn at crazy angles (her eyesight isn't too good these days) smudged bright red lipstick, and is dripping with heavy gold jewellery. Her boudoir is crammed with paintings and photographs of the rich and famous, and her enormous antique bed, the heart of her empire, holds her phone, a fax machine, books, a bell for her maid, several pairs of large diamante glasses and a hand mirror. She owes her long life and vitality apparently to a friend named Jack Daniels.

From the boudoir she keeps an eye on what's going on. French windows open onto a terrace and the swimming pool. She can eavesdrop on conversations and watch us swimming, but against the bright sunlight it's impossible to see inside. We only enter when summoned. It might be to chat about what we're reading, or about a piece of news. Sometimes she'll give advice about where to go and what to do, or more importantly, who to meet.

The dinner party, with bankers, politicians, and a couple of professors of fine art, yielded so many amazing invitations that we were instantly absorbed into Florentine high life. Our fortnight passed in a social whirl of sunning on the terraces of Medici villas, sipping *aperitivi* at sunset surrounded by fireflies, and eating and dancing under the stars at the local wild boar and porcini festivals.

We met a couple of Scandinavians at the dinner party. They'd bought some land and a farmhouse nearby because they'd always wanted to own a vineyard. We went to their place for *aperitivi,* and little by little their sorry tale emerged, which explained why they were trying to sell us their house. People in colder climes don't really understand the business of growing grapes. As a rule of thumb, if there are no vines there already, it's for a reason, and it's foolish to plant them. However, the Jensens had planted several acres which all failed because they were on a north-facing slope. Undaunted, they set about their next grand plan. It was to breed rabbits. You'd imagine that Swedes would have a better idea about rearing rabbits, but you'd be wrong. The little creatures simply burrowed their way under the fences and escaped. By this time, apparently, the locals were finding their escapades very funny, and awaited the next project with eager anticipation. It was to be a pear orchard. A goodly sum was invested in pear trees which were planted in straight rows, and which in the fullness of time, bore fruit. Sadly, this too was not a success. In this rather untamed landscape there are lots of wild boars. (Along every little lane you'll see notices saying hunting is forbidden and you'll see little vans parked whilst their owners sneak off into the woods to shoot their prey.) Now wild boars are very partial to pears, and they are sophisticated enough to have found a way of feeding on them in great quantities. They wait until dusk, then invade the orchards, butting the trees so that the fruit falls to the ground. No doubt it flavours the meat rather well, but it's not very good for the grower's budget.

We met the Jensen family at this desperate point in their Italian adventure. We certainly couldn't consider buying their house and land, even for the knock-down price. But luck was for once on their side. Mr Jensen needed to find employment since they had no revenue from their land, and shortly afterwards he managed to get the Coca Cola franchise for northern Tuscany. Their problems were over.

The Signora was scornful about the Jensens' naïve approach to living in her area, even though she kept them on her favoured guest list. She was horrified that we might have been tempted to buy the property. As the queen bee of that part of Tuscany, she expected everyone in her circle to defer to her superior knowledge.

"Look, daahlings," she drawled. "You need to know the right people and ask the right questions." They clearly hadn't achieved the Grand Dame's high standards of social etiquette.

Stefano, her faithful retainer, kept leaving us presents of newly laid eggs, and booked us into tiny local restaurants we'd never have found by ourselves. They all knew the American signora and gave us preferential rates as well as extra bottles of wine and olive oil to take away with us. Her favourite restaurant, il Cinghiale, was up in the hills at the end of a ten mile gravel track. As is often the case in Italy, you think you must be on the wrong road, miles from anywhere, as you drive through clouds of dust higher and ever higher, then suddenly you see a large full car park and you know that there are people feasting inside the rustic building. What worried me a little, when I thought about it, was that the staff at the Cinghiale kept a store of Jack Daniels for our hostess who still occasionally drove herself up there, and, of course, well lubricated, drove back again.

Erratic though her driving was, especially on the downward run, she was immune from prosecution. The *carabinieri* were in her pocket, and we were beneficiaries. They let us off a parking ticket when they realised where we were staying.

"Oh, no, signori. Friends of the American signora are friends of ours." The policeman waved a brilliantly white glove to dismiss us. "Just don't do it again."

The signora's dog was a large Alsatian called Wotan. When she was away from the heat of a Tuscan summer in her mountain home in Austria, Wotan lived in a compound near the farmhouse, looked after by Stefano, but when she was in residence Wotan roamed free to keep her company and protect her.

"Don't you worry about him, daahlings", she would reassure us. "He's a sweetie. He wouldn't hurt a fly."

All the same, we tended to give him a wide berth because he started howling and barking long before we ever got anywhere near him, and if we did approach, he growled menacingly, with gloopy strings of saliva dangling from his jaws. Some days we hardly dared venture towards the swimming pool which he seemed to be guarding with angry zeal. You'd hear her shout "Wotan!" from inside the villa, and he'd slink away, but somehow we knew that he'd quite fancy a taste of English flesh.

One morning all hell broke loose on the slope opposite the villa. Stefano and his two grown-up sons were shouting and yelling at Wotan who faced them snarling with a baby deer in his mouth. Stefano prized his jaws open whilst the others held him still and we watched from the safety of our terrace. The faun was dead, of course, but it wasn't going to be wasted. They skinned it and took it away for a feast. Our worst fears had been confirmed. Wotan was to be avoided at all costs.

Speaking of feasts, the signora recommended that we should examine notices pinned to tree trunks in the area.

"Look for the word *sagra,* daahlings. It means a village feast with whatever their speciality is. Could be chestnuts, could be wild boar…You can't go wrong."

Borgo San Lorenzo was having a *tortellini sagra* that week. (Rather like little cushions filled with mashed potato. More delicious than it sounds.) A marquee had been set up in the main piazza, and lots of stalls with local produce and other attractions lined the streets, such as the tombola stall you'll find at every *sagra.* (Tip: sometimes you just have to buy a numbered ticket, but where skill is involved, throwing a hoop to win a prize, you can always practise with the rubber rings from Kilner jars. That way you stand a chance of winning the good bottles of wine.)

The menu was pinned to the entrance of the marquee, and inside was the noisy sound of a hundred Italians doing what they enjoy most, eating and drinking. There were trestle tables covered in sheets of white paper and set out in rows with bread, water and wine at regular intervals. You placed your order, paid in advance and found a space. It was very popular, with hardly any free seats, but we at last sat down with a group of young locals, five youths who looked as if they'd come straight from the harvest with bits of straw still in their hair, and a plump girl with a squint who didn't say much but smiled all the time. They grinned at us, shuffled up a little to make more space, and passed us bread and wine. We seemed to be included in their chattering, but we couldn't understand the thick dialect. It became apparent that the girl held a special position within the group. They all constantly fondled her, fed her morsels, and patted her approvingly whenever she ventured to speak with her mouth full. We came to the only possible conclusion in view of such widespread intimacy that she was shared by all of them and gave her favours willingly, delighted to be their pet.

The groping, no doubt helped by the wine, grew more intimate as the meal progressed. It was something of a relief for us to move away from the table and saunter over to the space where dancing had begun. There was an accordion, a violin, a guitar and drums, and the dancing was old-fashioned and wholesome. Our group of young peasants seemed to have constant difficulty establishing whose turn it was to dance with their floozie. She waited patiently for them to sort it out, and was led round the dance floor, being fondled the whole time. Eventually the impatience of those waiting their turn was too much to bear. They all danced with her in one big tight circle, and she dreamily smiled from one to the next, accepting their embraces and swaying to the rhythm.

We were summoned to the royal presence in the boudoir the next day to report back on our adventures. The Grand Dame wanted to know if we had plans to go to Florence to do some real dining instead of the peasant stuff. We stood there, awkwardly dripping as we'd come straight from the pool. She rang a bell for Francesca to come and give us extra towels to stand on, so we knew we were there for a while. Wotan snarled jealously, but she told him firmly to stop and threw a couple of biscuits to join the debris of bones around the floor to distract him from tasty wet English ankles.

Yes, we were planning to take the train to Florence in a couple of days.

"Well, daahlings, you simply must go eat at my favourite restaurant. Let me find their card. Where is it? I can't remember a thing these days. I'm falling apart. Bless you, daahling, would you find it for me?"

I was instructed to pass over an elaborately carved box standing on the chest of drawers opposite her gigantic bed. The box was full of cards and mementoes which she rifled through with her gnarled hands, heavy with large gold rings and varnished with bright red nails, until she found hat she was looking for.

"*Ecco ci qua*!" she exclaimed. Her Italian was good, but with a pronounced American accent.

We hadn't actually planned an expensive exclusive lunch in Florence, but we felt we couldn't turn down her suggestion. She picked up her bedside phone and booked us a table, then explained where the restaurant was, although it was probably at least a decade since she'd eaten there. These days she can just about walk around the villa with a stick on one side and Wotan on the other. A city would be out of the question.

Ristorante da Mario was quite a walk from the centre. We were greeted like royalty since the American signora had booked for us, and ushered to the best table with great flourishes and flicking of napkins. No menu was offered. They had their instructions to serve us their specialities.

"Here, sir and madam," said our waiter as he set our *primo piatto* before us. He seemed to wish to speak to us in English, but we wondered if the dish he announced as *tagliolini with dormouses* had been a little lost in translation. Good, all the same. Our first tentative tiny forkfuls were followed by shovelling it in and we soon demolished the first course. The *secondo piatto* was wheeled in on a trolley. It looked very impressive, but not, perhaps, as something to eat: more an interesting installation. We each had a large white plate, in the middle of which stood a chicken's head, surveying us with beady eyes. Arranged around it were circles of its stuffed neck like so many slices of salami. A light salad was recommended to accompany Little Red Hen. I turned her away so that she couldn't watch me whilst I tried eating her neck. I wasn't sure whether the head was edible or not, but I couldn't imagine there was much meat on it.

I chewed my way through my main course without much enthusiasm, rather reluctantly turning the head on its side to cut off what little meat there was on it. Other diners seemed to have picked theirs up and were gnawing them with gusto.

So much for Italian cuisine being pizza and pasta.

At the end of the most amazing two weeks, we went across to the signora's villa to thank her before heading off back to Montebello.

"Well, daahlings," she said. "I know how you love your part of Italy. I just wanted you to enjoy *my* special part of Italy before my deadline. I may be in the departure lounge, but I haven't departed yet."

8.   TRATTORIA TIPS

Many Italophiles will already be familiar with the adventures of Inspector Montalbano in the detective novels of Andrea Camilleri, set in Sicily. A good third of every story is usually devoted to the meals the hero consumes, described in mouth-watering detail, course by course, almost mouthful by savoured mouthful. Nothing could better enable the reader to enter the Inspector's world, his inner thoughts and needs, and of course in this respect he is typical of all his fellow countrymen. When the stories appear as films on TV, the time devoted to eating is drastically reduced, presumably because viewers want to get on with the action, but the balanced world of eating and catching criminals goes on reassuringly in every new book. Inspector Montalbano has his priorities right. When a colleague asks him for dinner and he knows the wife can't cook, he tells lies to avoid going there. When his favourite restaurant on the coast closes down, he mopes around the empty tables until the owner comes out and promises to cook again, just once more, for him.

And so it is throughout the land. For poor peasants and rich city dwellers alike, good meals are the important punctuation marks of daily life in Italy. Skipping lunch would be unthinkable. Patronising a take-away establishment is only OK if it's a pizza place with a 20 year reputation for excellence. Chains of mediocre restaurants are unheard of. The thousands of *ristoranti* and *trattorie* cooking fantastic food twice a day six days a week are family owned and run, and form the basis of that home-from-home hospitality that nobody does better than the Italians.

There is really no such thing as Italian food. Each region has its own specialities which you won't be able to find anywhere else unless a family has moved, say, from Lombardy to Lazio. Even the bread differs enormously. Tuscan bread has a very hard crust, and has no salt in it, dating proudly back to a time many centuries ago when Florence was under siege and there was no salt to be had. In Piedmont the bread is soft and delicious, often served warm, whilst in the Veneto the pale *panini* are all shaped by hand, resembling Cornish pasties. I have a particular fondness for *pinzin*, a speciality bread from Ferrara. (I've never seen it anywhere else.) This bread comes in piping hot puffed up triangles, deep fried, and is so delicious that I'm usually too full to enjoy my meal by the time the first course is served.

Pasta also varies from region to region. In southern Italy you'll find *orechiette*, little ear-shaped pasta; *strozza preti* (strangled priests) in Umbria; and *bigoli,* like fat spaghetti, in my part of the Veneto. In Friuli risotto rice is often replaced by barley (*orzotto*) and you'll never eat *arancini,* (meaning little oranges, but actually savoury rice balls), outside Sicily.

Lunch is for many Italians the main meal of the day. It begins later than ours, and often continues until four o'clock or even later. We were once driving through the flat rice fields of Lombardy, on our way to Montebello and very hungry, at about two in the afternoon. The landscape was empty and uninteresting, not the sort of country where you expect to find a decent place to eat. We'd almost given up hope of finding anywhere when we turned a corner and saw a farmhouse surrounded by about 50 cars.

"Got to be a restaurant," was the verdict, and we pulled in.

It turned out to be a wedding reception, but we were not turned away. Instead we were invited to join in, and offered all sorts of regional delicacies to try until we were stuffed to the gills. The best of the many dishes was of course rice-based. It was a kind of risotto which had then been fried to make a cake with a crisp golden base.

Good old Italian hospitality! We became part of the family and spent the rest of the afternoon and evening being pressed to eat, drink, dance and be merry, giving up on our plans to get to the Veneto by nightfall.

On another trek across the North Italian Plain we found ourselves driving along the Via Emilia in August. It was getting late and every place we passed through had virtually closed down for the summer. Spotting a sign pointing down a lane to our left, we drove to the Molino Bianco. It was indeed (or had been) a white windmill and to our relief it was open and a room was available. The room, naturally, was completely round. What was odd was that its walls were lined with green baize. It was like sleeping inside a rolled up snooker table. A fan on the ceiling jostled the stagnant air around a bit, but it was still uncomfortably hot and humid. The local *trattoria* was closed, and the cook in the Molino was on holiday, so we needed advice about where to eat.

No problem of course. We followed instructions and walked down the lane to where a group of old men were playing cards outside a house. Inside was a large table laid out with floured freshly-made pasta, and beyond was another room with a smaller table.

"Come in, come in." The lady of the house ushered us forward and told us what she would prepare for us. What a feast! Local salami, home made pasta (of course), roast stuffed rabbit and large bowls of fresh fruit floating in iced water to keep it cool. And all for about £5 each, including their own soft fruity wine.

At this point I feel a pronouncement coming on. *You'll hardly ever find a bad restaurant in Italy.* There are plenty of better-than-average ones, yes, but if you want to eat fantastically well, here are some tips so that you can sample the very best that Italy has to offer, and it won't break the bank.

1. Don't be misled by appearances.

Many wonderful restaurants are distinctly shabby on the outside. Rather like some of Italy's most famous churches, it's as if they've never quite got round to finishing off the exterior because what matters is inside. Your restaurant will be even better if it actually doesn't look like an eating place at all. Typically, you might have to walk through someone's living room, and *nonna* (grandma) will be cooking at the back.

One of the best meals we ever had in Venice was in just such a place, and very pleased we were to find it, because Venice can be disappointing and expensive on the food front for the unsuspecting tourist. We had an address, but of course that didn't mean we'd be able to find it, because Venice has the most bewildering addresses in the world. All you have is the name of the *sestiere*, one of the six divisions of the city, and a number which can be in the thousands. A Venetian address never includes street names. You can wander round for hours, thinking you might be close to your destination, only to find that the number sequence doesn't continue around the next corner and you're back in the hundreds again.

For this restaurant, the Dante, even the locals couldn't decide where it was. They have a notebook where they can look up such things, but I've never seen this book for sale. I think it's a conspiracy to keep non-residents in a state of confusion.

Anyway, footsore and very hungry, we eventually found our place for lunch and rather uncertainly walked into what appeared to be a scruffy small shop selling a few scraps of fish. The rotund signor behind the counter waved us through to his garden at the back where three tables we set for lunch. He then proceeded to inform us what we were having, and very delicious it was too.

Which brings me to my next tip.

2. Choose restaurants with no menu and eat what you're told.

Of course you need to be quite confident to try this, but even with very limited Italian, they will appreciate your efforts and try to explain what's on offer. After all, they just want you to enjoy the experience of eating at their place. Small family run restaurants won't necessarily have anything ready prepared, especially out of season, and you may have a bit of a wait.

At one place on the Amalfi coast in March we were ushered to a table, offered some wine and asked if we fancied some fish. When we agreed, the man got on his bike and came back 10 minutes later with a parcel of sea bass under his arm.

This was cooked to perfection in the way he recommended, and we dined royally in an otherwise empty restaurant.

When we first went to the little trattoria in Montebello we didn't understand what we were being offered. What on earth was spaghetti with *musso*? The waiter waved the cook over to our table. He came out of the kitchen, put his fingers up on each side of his head and said, "He haw, he haw!" We got the message, and actually donkey meat sauce on pasta is OK even when you realise what it is.

The famous jolly meal with the Presidente, where I got thoroughly tipsy, (chapter 1) included several plates of deep fried *fiori di zucca*. I had never seen these before, but tucked in with gusto as they very nicely complimented the *prosecco*. These fried flowers brought out with a flourish by the chef-owner of the Belvedere have now become my all time favourite antipasto.

3. Eat where the locals eat regularly.

As Italians are so very choosy about where they eat, it makes sense to eat where they do. Don't be put off by a drive of several miles along an unsurfaced road, a *strada bianca*, to find a recommended restaurant. You might think you're completely lost, but then you'll turn a corner and see a full car park.

Even better, possibly, is when you spot the favourite lunch time haunts of workmen. The Quadrifoglio is a *trattoria* where we eat regularly, up in the Euganean Hills in the small village of Teolo. Almost every lunchtime you'll see a fire engine outside, taking up virtually all the available parking space in the small main square. All the local firemen will be sitting at a rectangular table eating the *menu fisso* three course menu of the day. They have their mobile phones displayed prominently on the table, but somehow, like Inspector Montalbano, putting out a fire won't be a priority for the fire brigade if it coincides with a delicious meal. Duty may call, but duty can wait. Incidentally, the copious portions served in this place are far too much for mere tourists to get through. Another tip here would be to ask for one menu to be shared between two people. Don't worry; they do it all the time.

Most Italians treat their local restaurant as home from home. In Testaccio, a working class area of central Rome, you can find *trattorie* patronised by the same people almost every day of the week. (The menus there are almost always based on offal because of the proximity of an immense slaughterhouse, now a gallery space, the *Mattatoio*.) The regular customers don't stand on ceremony: when most customers have left, they walk around the tables draining all the bottles and glasses, enjoying weird cocktails to finish their meal.

4. Avoid menus in English and twee checked tablecloths.

Of course this is easier said than done if you happen to be in Florence, for instance, or Lake Garda, but as a rule of thumb, don't go to the obvious places on the main drag. The back lanes will be full of places not so obviously pretty, but with much more authentic food. If you encounter waiters touting for business on the street, as you might in a more touristy place, this can only mean that they don't have much of a reputation and locals certainly won't be eating there. Candles, especially if stuck in Chianti bottles, checked tablecloths and giant pepper mills are also obviously to be avoided. Such places depend on passing trade: they don't expect their customers to return.

5. Look for the "Fatal Flaw"

Over the years I've come to notice that every really good Italian restaurant has something small wrong with it, almost as if to avoid absolute perfection. Many is the time we've come across a live wire sticking out of a hole in the ceiling, or a crudely written note stuck with duct tape to the wash basins in the otherwise elegant loo, telling us not to waste water. The flaw will never be anything to do with the food, but it will certainly be there, in a classy place where you wouldn't expect it. There are often lots of really good paintings on the walls, and then you'll spot a real piece of framed kitsch, a Disney child with a tear trickling down its cheek perhaps, or a rather suspect female nude with more to do with lust than art.

In Ferrara there's a restaurant with a little outdoor terrace for summer, which has a wire coming down the wall from an upstairs window, attached to an extension lead, then joined to wires connecting with chandeliers under each parasol. The plugs and sockets are exposed to the elements. I haven't seen what happens when it rains. The beautiful *ristorante* at Piazzola sul Brenta, with a terrace facing the sublime Villa Contarini has cracked marble stairs at the entrance, protected, or maybe even held together, by duct tape and polythene sheeting.

Even Michelin recommended restaurants in Italy can have something a bit odd about them, though I shouldn't go so far as to label them flawed. There's one in Castelfranco with a ceiling hung with hundreds of handbags. It proved to be only a small diversion however, compared with the couple on the next table who seemed more likely to devour each other than their meal. I've seen similar themes in Abano (baseball caps), Dogliani (giant cartoons of Andy Capp, oddly enough) Rome (a shrine to Ferrari), and Orvieto (model chickens), and that's apart from the clichéd decorations of fishing nets and star fish which adorn a lot of seafood restaurants. (But these are also likely to have checked tablecloths and candles in bottles. See 4 above.)

6. Remember, "da" means "chez"

It came as a sudden revelation to me a few years ago that so many restaurants in Italy are called "da" something or other. (For instance, we regularly go to a superb place in Rome called Da Vincenzo, and another in Torreglia called Da Tapparo.) "Da" literally means "at the home of", just like the French equivalent, "chez". It's yet another clear indication of a restaurant owned and run by a family where the service is personal, they remember regular customers and take a pride in the quality of their meals.

7. Look at the chef.

Opposite the municipio in Montebello is a rather run down *trattoria* where the old codgers gather during the day to sip red wine and chat at the outside tables. It's the sort of place with no menu but there are two things in its favour. One is that it's usually busy in the evening, and the other is that the chef is almost spherical. A well-respected chef once told me that he always looks into the kitchen before dining anywhere, and if the chef is thin, he doesn't stay.

For two glorious weeks in April this little place serves the greatest delicacy in the Veneto. A particular kind of crab is caught at Chioggia on the Venetian lagoon. They are called *moleche* in dialect (nobody seems to be able to give me their official name) and shed their shells each spring, slowly growing another one. Meanwhile the creatures are eaten whole, after soaking them in beaten egg, of which they absorb a surprising amount, and fried in oil. It is like crunching though fish-flavoured *Twiglets,* and is savoured, almost worshipped, by the locals. I had no idea then of the symbolic importance of these crabs to the Venetian lagoon, but all will be explained in chapter 13.

The little *trattoria* goes crazy at this time. The tables are all pushed together, with jugs of bubbling *prosecco* at regular intervals, and mounds of deep fried *moleche* are brought in, served with polenta. I ate there last spring and looked at these plates with envy. You have to be in the know and order them in advance because they're quite expensive and also quite hard to come by. I know better now!

8. Consult guide books and go for local snacks in tourist cities

It's always harder to find good authentic restaurants in the big cities frequented by tourists in large numbers. It pays to do your homework and consult a good guide book so that you won't be disappointed or ripped off. As an alternative it's often sensible to buy or take sandwiches and leave your main meal until the evening where with any luck you may be staying a little off the beaten track. Better still, find out about local snack places. For instance in Venice you can buy snacks called *cicchetti,* similar to tapas, for about 1 Euro each. You'll find them in bars called *bacari* where you usually stand to eat.

9. Always look for the sign of the snail.

The Slow Food Movement, opposing fast food, was invented by the Italians (in the suitably uplifting town of Bra) and has spread throughout Italy and beyond in the past ten years. Briefly, the philosophy is good quality local food cooked freshly on the premises, and its symbol, appropriately enough, is a snail. Check the door of your intended restaurant and if there's a snail sticker, go in immediately. You will never be disappointed.

10. Don't be seduced by a historic setting.

On a recent trip to Ferrara, our favourite restaurant, Ca' d' Frara was closed. We wandered aimlessly around the *centro storico* until we came upon the Brindisi, a restaurant apparently patronised in its early days by such celebrities as Copernicus. The proud boast was that it was still serving the original mediaeval menu.

We decided to give it a try. This was not a good idea. When the main course came, it looked rather like the square pincushions I used to make out of felt in junior school, except that the neat blanket stitch surrounded a surface of pink steaming pig skin. The knives we were supplied with made no impression. I tried stabbing mine with a fork, whereupon it shot off my plate on to Phil's knee. He had more success with his fork, and made a hole from which emerged a slow fountain of melted fat which continued for several seconds. The cushion's contents tasted rather good, spicy minced meat with dried fruit, but I wouldn't say the experience of hard wooden benches and basic ancient recipes was worth repeating however enthusiastic the staff and however historic the building.

11. Opt for a local or seasonal menu

Italian friends always stare in disbelief at the array of unseasonal fruits and vegetables in our supermarkets in England. They just know that if it isn't freshly and locally grown it will have no flavour. Which is why you need to be aware of regional dishes and whatever is in season.

In our area, the best local asparagus comes from Pernumia. Don't let April pass in the Veneto without sampling it. When in Treviso, in early spring be sure to sample its radicchio, a red long leaved cabbage, often served in pasta dishes. There are hundreds of other local and seasonal specialities: you'll never sample them all in one lifetime. The Antica Trattoria dei Paccagnella in Padua is run by a genial enthusiast called Cesare, who has grown rather more portly over the years. Having eaten there a few times, we recently found ourselves admitted to his inner circle and invited to a seasonal tasting evening. It began at 8.30, but once the shops had closed we decided to go straight there and sample the *aperitivi.* By the time the other diners arrived, we were already on to our second bottle of *serprino,* even though there was to be a different wine with each of the five courses. It was of course a magnificent evening, themed around the flavours of autumn. We sampled shavings of Alba truffles on a tartare antipasto, pasta medallions stuffed with chestnut and ricotta in pheasant sauce, a delicate lasagnetta with pumpkin and sausage, roast wild boar with pine nuts and mushrooms, and a beautiful chocolate and vanilla mousse decorated with seasonal fruits. How do I remember all this? Well, apart from being totally memorable, I kept the menu. Cesare had moved all the tables into long rows so that the diners all sat together and chatted noisily. We were with a male nurse and a man from the fire brigade, with their respective spouses.

The nurse painted views of Padua in his spare time, whilst the fireman grew his own vegetables in his *orto*.

It would be a mistake to consider that in Italy, as in much of England, food is merely fuel. It is so much more. It is at the centre of everything Italians hold dear, and of everything we love about Italy. It is at the heart of the warm generosity of Italian hospitality, the "home from home" atmosphere of every *trattoria*. You always sense the need of the owners to ensure that you are enjoying their food, their drink and their establishment. They offer you their freshest ingredients cooked according to handed-down family recipes, and their pleasure in serving you will equal yours in enjoying every mouthful. So keen are they to make your meal a fantastic experience that they are often reluctant to let you go. Just when you've asked for *il conto*, a tray of *limoncello* appears *in omaggio* (with the compliments of the management) and the warm glow it induces stays with you as you stagger out beaming and wend your way along the street.

9. STRICTLY GRACE AND FLAVOUR: dancing with the ice cream maestro

It always happens in Italy. You spend a short time in a place, get to know people, and before you know it, you're part of the family and invited to their son's wedding next spring. Which is why we found ourselves being driven to the church in the next village to Montebello by a manic driver from Umbria called Luigi, uncle of the bride. In all other respects Luigi is a very amiable man, but put him behind the wheel of a motor and he imagines he's driving a Ferrari. The only good thing about that drive, apart from arriving surprisingly in one piece, was his absolute insistence that when we were next in Orvieto, we had to go to the best ice cream parlour in Italy, Pasqualetti's.

As it happens, we have a couple of dear Italian friends who live near Orvieto, whom we visit about once a year. We were planning on going there again that summer to organise a painting group which Phil was to tutor and I was to play matron. (That's the next chapter.) It's a long journey from and to Montebello in the middle of a heat wave, especially in my car, the Silver Snail, which is without air conditioning, but it's always worth the journey. By the time we reach Orvieto we're usually dripping and bad tempered, but the breeze as you climb up the steep rocks to the old walled city in the funicular railway, together with the prospect of heavenly ice cream, always revives us.

The *gelateria* in Orvieto wasn't hard to find, following Luigi's advice: it's in the main square to the left of the magnificent cathedral. A couple of *carabinieri* were taking an ice cream break in the doorway, and all around the piazza satisfied customers were licking away as melted ice cream trickled down their wrists. Pasqualetti's is ice cream heaven. There are framed reviews and prize certificates on every wall, and they were advertising their special seasonal flavours. Is there any wonder that Italians eat giant cones (ask for a *maxi cono*) with balls of so many different colours and flavours squashed into them? It's so hard to choose. I opted for white fig, even though my favourite pink grapefruit ice cream was on offer, and Phil chose pine nut ice cream.

We took our ice creams to a small piazza round the back of the cathedral and sat on some steps, contentedly licking away rapidly in the hot sunshine before they melted. The piazza was practically deserted, shutters closed against the bright light and a hint of a breeze stirring the geraniums in their pots on windowsills.

Suddenly Phil jumped to his feet and ran across the cobbles chasing a small piece of paper. He grabbed it and walked back towards me, waving the paper with a big grin on his face.

"Look at this!" he exclaimed, "It's a 50 euro note. Where did it come from?

We looked all around. Nobody. Should we keep it?

A group of teenagers sauntered round the corner looking at us and grinning. We had a hasty discussion.

"Do you think it's theirs? They look as if they know about it."

A bit reluctantly, we decided to ask if they'd lost a 50 euro note. Yes, they said. We were very kind to return it. We weren't so sure, but after all we'd lost nothing, so we consoled ourselves by giving in to temptation and went back for another ice cream.

We were staying in an *agriturismo* run by our friends in the hills nearby. (These are converted farm buildings which accommodate guests – very comfortably - and feed them superbly on their own produce.) I mentioned to our friend the divine Marco, who manages the place, that we'd discovered Pasqualetti's. He gave me a significant look, but said nothing.

I need to explain – or should I say eulogise – about Marco. He is an Italian Adonis, so handsome that it's difficult if you're female not to swoon in his presence, especially if he puts a hand on your shoulder. (He's a tactile person.) He could have stepped out of a fresco by Piero della Francesca. Yes, he really is that gorgeous. When for instance we once asked his advice about hiring a car from Orvieto station, he suggested the Hertz office because he knew Silvia who would give us a discount. Of course Silvia provided the *sconto,* dreamily telling us that Marco was a god.

On another occasion, we'd left the Silver Snail in his care for a week whilst we'd gone off by train to Rome, then returned to pick up the car again. Marco had warned us about the birds which had a taste for rubber and were very fond of eating windscreen wipers, so I'd encased the wipers in plastic bags. The car had thoughtfully been moved to the shade of a mulberry tree for the time we were away in Rome. When we next saw it, it was covered with masses purple sticky stains, some pure fruit, and others which had rather disgustingly been processed by the birds. But we'd forgotten about the rubber seal which surrounded the sun roof. When we finally managed to wipe off some of the thick purple mess, we noticed that the sun roof now had a scalloped border where a whole flock of birds had been pecking away. It didn't rain the whole time we were there, so it was impossible to know whether it was still waterproof.

But I digress. Back at the *agriturismo* that evening a notice went up outside the dining room where the menu was displayed. We were informed that tomorrow's feast would be something to do with "*La Grotta*" which we didn't quite understand.

"Bound to be good whatever it is," was the general consensus, so we were surprised that we were the only ones in the dining room the next evening. But Marco came to fetch us, and about 25 diners set off across the fields towards the setting sun with the Living God in the lead. We came to a log cabin which was unlocked with a flourish. Inside was an installation of cheeses, salamis and hams hanging from the rafters. Steps going down into darkness led to a maze of wine cellars.

Our first course was a general tasting of all this abundance, with explanations from Marco about the importance of their local organic produce, (they call it biological in Italian) and how his *agriturismo* was even more devoted to genuine local foods and flavours than the Slow Food Movement. We sat around on rustic wooden tables, bathed in the orange glow of the setting sun and drinking in the fantastic vista as well as the cabernet and *Orvieto Classico* on offer.

After the first course there followed a spirited staggering

back across the fields for the rest of the meal, arranged on the terrace outdoors with a local jazz trio to add to the atmosphere. The sun had set, and the terrace was lit with dozens of candles and small dishes of citronella to keep the flies at bay.

We recognised at a nearby table the same group of youngsters who claimed to have lost 50 euros that afternoon. They greeted us with handshakes all round and the fun of the evening began.

As he took my plate, Marco said he wanted to introduce me to someone. I followed him, and was quickly drawn in from a handshake into the arms of Signor Pasqualetti, the ice cream impresario in person, who needed a dance partner for the rest of the evening.

Not only does the man make the most delicious ice cream on the planet. He also happens to be the best dance partner I've ever had; the kind who, with slight pressure on the shoulder blade, can guide you to perform dances you've never heard of as if you've been doing it all your life. He's a small dapper man of about 65, immaculately dressed in a lightweight suit, and with a benign smile on his face because dancing and ice cream are what he loves best in the whole world. We sashayed from end to end and corner to corner in front of the tables, and when he danced the shoes off my feet (literally) he carried on pirouetting alone across the cobbles whilst I fastened the straps on my red sandals again to come back for more.

At some point I returned to our table for a drink and noticed a 50 euro note on my chair. Instantly, I looked towards the teenagers who were watching and laughing, motioning me to turn the note over. On the back the word SPECIMEN appeared in large letters. The joke was on us. The kids said they often played this trick on tourists to see how honest they were. At least we'd improved the score for *inglesi.*

The night was young and needed to be danced away. I became a bit concerned to be monopolising Signor Pasqualetti who'd been sitting with a rather strange looking woman with dyed blond hair and thick black eyebrows. She was looking decidedly menacing, and glaring in my direction.

"Don't worry," Marco reassured me. "She's just a gold-digger after his ice cream fortune because he's a widower. Anyway, she can't dance."

I tripped back across the terrace to join the dancing maestro.

We were invited back to the ice cream *laboratorio* the next day. It was in the mediaeval cellars under the shop, a sweet-smelling sticky place where the many fridges gave out hot fumes as they struggled to keep the produce chilled. On every surface there were pyramids of fruits being weighed, and tubs of cream standing next to sacks of sugar on the floor. There could be no dispute: this was real ice cream made with real ingredients. Large ladies in white overalls stirred the vats, up to their elbows in pastel-coloured ice creams. Signor Pasqualetti darted about gracefully with giant wooden ladles and big metal spoons, inviting us to try all the different flavours (about 30 at a guess).

And so, when I'm at home on a cool autumn day, I transport myself to Umbria from Northumbria, and dream of a balmy summer's feast in the hills. When I cross the road in Montebello for my daily ration of a tub of liquirizia ice cream, I always remember waltzing across the cobblestones with Maestro Pasqualetti. And with the promise of free ice cream for life, I go back there every year. Time after time I say to myself that my Italian experiences can't be beaten, but delights always follow delights in Italy. I'm never disappointed.

10. PAINTING BY NUMBERS: The trials and tribulations of organising a painting group in Italy

Waiting at Orvieto station for yet another Rome train which failed to disgorge the remaining four ladies of our painting group, I began to regret ever taking on the task of organising the painting week in Umbria. Phil runs an adult art class throughout the winter months in Newcastle, and we had the idea a couple of years ago that the group might like to team up with another, run by one of Phil's ex students, now a professional artist, and paint in Italy for a week. Luckily, our friends in Umbria run the best little *agriturismo* for miles around, and we were able to accommodate our budding artists there. We'd driven down the *autostrada* a couple of days earlier from Montebello to set things up. It was my job to make all the arrangements, and I was already feeling not a little put-upon.

It was very hot indeed. Up to now, everything had gone smoothly. Three of our number had come all the way from England by train without a hitch, two had driven, and three had flown from Luton to Ciampino. The two who'd come from the north of England by car had hardly known each other before they set off in Sally's open top sports car. They'd had a few disagreements along the way, mainly because Sally, in her variety of jaunty hats and large sunglasses was constantly tooted at and flirted with, whereas her companion was appalled at all the attention they'd received. However, they were all now happily enjoying the landscape over a glass of wine.

The other four's whereabouts remained a mystery. We had contact numbers but they weren't answering. Their Easyjet flight from Newcastle had apparently landed on time, and we couldn't think what else to do but wait.

I had visions of a *Tea with Mussolini*-type scene in Rome's Termini station where they'd become embroiled in a mini-drama with the *carabinieri* because they hadn't validated their rail tickets by punching them in the little yellow machine. I could quite see Barbara wielding her umbrella, Maggie Smith style, whilst delivering a lecture on how we don't need to validate tickets in England.

Back at the *agriturismo*, we were somewhat consoled by a magnificent evening meal of mixed antipasti, asparagus pasta, pheasant with truffles and *semifreddo*, all made on the premises from their own produce and served by Marco, our friend and the most beautiful young man with impeccable manners whom everyone came to adore. The sun slipped dramatically behind the rolling hills bathing us all in a rosy pink glow, greatly helped by the food and wine. It was tempting to forget about our missing colleagues.

However, duty called. Pooling information, we found the home number of one of the missing ladies and tried it without much hope of success.

"Hello," said Diane chirpily. "I've almost finished packing."

And now I know the Italian word for FLABBERGASTED (*sbalordito*), because that's what I was.

With surprising efficiency, I'd supplied all the group

members with a detailed information pack about the place; costs, times, and *above all* dates. But these dames had got it into their heads that the week was Sunday to Sunday, and not Saturday to Saturday. There was nothing to do but spend the next afternoon at the station again to meet the Rome train. We trundled down the hill again. The trees and barns which bordered the winding lane were beginning to look extremely familiar. The waiter in the station bar greeted us like old friends: after all, we'd become very good customers.

I smiled grimly when they arrived, telling myself anyone could make such a mistake and we mustn't let it spoil the week. After all, last year in Tuscany had been a huge success.

Well, almost. There was the time when our least talented painter had nearly been run over by a tractor. Typically, she'd set up an expensive array of tubes of paint, brushes, bottles and rags along a low wall at the edge of the farm track, and positioned her easel in the middle of the lane to get the best view of the picturesque farm buildings and vineyard beyond. Stefano came chugging round the corner on his tractor, hardly prepared for such an obstacle, and stopped only just in time. The easel came crashing down in her shock to get out of the way, and pots and brushes were scattered everywhere. The rather beautiful patches of lichen are now enhanced by vivid orange and violet splashes.

On another occasion we'd all decided to go for a pizza and booked a table for 18 outside on the pavement. Two of our number decided we were too near the road and wanted the staff to move everything indoors. They were overruled. Then there was Lizzie who refused to sleep in the room next to the cupboard where spare artists' materials were kept. Maybe she had a point: there was also a complete skeleton on a stand in there. Dennis, who'd never travelled abroad before, found it difficult to come to terms with the fact that the rooms were kept so dark all day, and complained that the towels were like dish cloths. He also seemed to attract every biting insect in the vicinity, and his white legs, displayed below rather short shorts, became increasingly mottled as the week progressed.

But as I say, the previous year in the gorgeous landscape of Tuscany had been a great success, which was why we were doing it again in the similarly sumptuous landscape of Umbria.

The thing was, now that everyone was happily installed, to ensure smooth running from now on.

Monday was glorious. After the briefing they pottered about with their folding chairs, sun hats and easels choosing the perfect spot in the olive groves, or looking at the fading textures of the old walls of tumble-down barns. There was an atmosphere of enthusiasm, wanting to get started.

I sighed blissfully and withdrew into my book by the pool. My weeks of planning had ended and I deserved a little bit of "me time". I'd just reached that moment in my luxurious inner debate about whether to swim when I'd finished my chapter, when I heard a voice close by.

"Myra. Can you help me?"

It was Brenda, the miscreant who'd bought the four plane tickets for the wrong day. She rummaged inside her copious canvas bag and produced a light bulb, explaining that it wasn't bright enough to read by at night. Having a little experience of remote hill farms in Italy and their unreliable electricity supply, I tried to explain gently that it might not be possible without blowing all the fuses, and returned to my book. This was a rural idyll, not the Umbria Hilton.

But my antennae were alerted. I next came upon an interesting scene on the terrace. Brenda had decided to order a bottle of wine, but insisted, in that loud English reserved for foreigners, on having only a bottle with a label on it so that she knew what she was drinking. The previous night, we'd had the *vino della casa*, and smooth and velvety-good it was too, but obviously not good enough for madam. A labelled bottle was found, and peace reigned again.

Most of the group had by now installed themselves in the neighbouring olive groves and fields, with improvised easels, boxes of equipment and bottles of water. Dennis, our talented watercolourist, here for a second stint after Tuscany, managed to catch a tic which burrowed into his inside thigh. ("Serve him right," I thought, "for wearing such short shorts.") Luckily, Anne, who was a retired doctor, had brought an entire medicine chest with her and performed the operation skilfully that evening whilst anxious colleagues looked on in admiration.

The weather for the rest of the week was a disaster. The magical fireflies which had so entranced us in Tuscany the year before had all gone to ground. The locals kept saying how exceptional it was, but it was small consolation. We didn't have enough sweaters and cardigans, and painting in the rain was a challenge too far. There were only two hire cars between us (they were fearful of mad Italian drivers), so we were stuck on top of the hill.

Anne did a beautiful charcoal self portrait standing in her nightie facing a full length mirror. David painted a layered grey landscape through the grille of his bedroom window. Jenny, a rather flighty younger woman on the rebound, hitched a lift down the hill in the postman's van, and came back drenched but happy with five pairs of sparkly sandals from the market at five euros a pair. When in no time the glass beads and sequins fell off her sandals, she incorporated them into a huge collage. Brenda didn't seem to do much at all. When we all met for the first review of the work in progress, she said she'd just have a cup of tea instead, and proceeded to lecture the uncomprehending staff on how to pour boiling water over tea instead of placing the tea bag in the saucer.

Holding "crits" on the terrace wasn't a good idea. There were awnings to protect us from the sun, or in this case, the wet weather, but the wind drove the rain at us sideways. We retired to the gym. The drawings and paintings were attached to the walls or to the various machines with masking tape until the whole area looked like an installation at Tate Modern. The giant collage of sequins, buttons and general souvenirs like bus tickets, leaflets and Italian debris snaked across the floor between a treadmill and a weight-lifting machine. We stepped carefully over it to admire each artist's work in turn.

Luckily the two tutors managed to convey enthusiasm, and the location did have points in its favour despite the weather. The food was fabulous, the wine (with or without labels) rich and fruity, and the manager, my friend Marco, was a living

Adonis. Straight out of a renaissance painting, he charmed the women with his dazzling smile and light friendly touches on the shoulder. We swooned in his presence.

It didn't occur to me until Friday that our four late-comers would need accommodation for Saturday night when the others had gone. Marco, with his usual unselfconscious eagerness to please, tried to find them a hotel in Rome. It was a national holiday: everything was booked. Eventually he found a place near Orvieto and volunteered to pick up a minibus and meet them at 6.30 the following morning to drive them and their luggage to the station. And this young god is single!

Marco distributed our bills with generous discounts. He clearly didn't realise that his smile was a marketable asset and he could have charged the females double without any complaints. Obviously the only person who queried the extras on the bill was Brenda. But even she couldn't spoil the camaraderie of the group.

And now they're all suggesting (with one exception) that I organise another one next year. I rather think I might. Federico the librarian has told me about an old monastery up the Euganean Hills near Montebello. The views are fantastic, and with his contacts it could be the gastronomic and visual experience of a lifetime. As long as Brenda doesn't come.

11. BLING AND MANGLED ENGLISH: the bad bag collection

It's a curious thing that Italian men always look good on big occasions whilst the women can often look like so many trollops. Everybody knows that Italian suits, especially Armani, are the best, and are shown to advantage by Italian male bodies. Italian women's bodies are equally beautiful, but they just don't need all that over-the-top decoration that they go in for. Heaven knows, Britain is populated by chavs and scrubbers who wear the most appalling outfits to enhance their lumpy bodies and tattoos. I'm discounting all of that. No, I'm talking about the trend-setters, the beautiful people with money to spend on stylish clothes.

Subtle or classic aren't concepts known to the signoras and signorinas I see everywhere. Why have a straight hem line when you can have one that dips up and down? Combine that with a slit to reveal as much thigh as possible and you'll have the must-have skirt of the season.

It's the same with tops; the more cleavage revealed, the better. Current fashion seems to dictate that *all* women should emphasise and reveal their curves, but in Italy it does seem a bit more extreme. They wear shirts that a decade ago would have been rejected as far too small. They are button-poppingly tight, with ovals of flesh exposed between the fastenings. I wonder how many mini explosions there are each day when the straining buttons finally give in and bountiful nature bursts free.

Female clothing is over-decorated too. Why would you want

sequins on a pair of jeans? Why do you need tee shirts that sparkle? Surely all that lovely sunshine is sufficient. It makes more sense for women in colder climes to seek out something to dazzle.

As for the jewellery… a chandelier hanging from each ear, and rows of sparkling chains and beads are *de rigueur*. "If you've got it, flaunt it," is their motto, whereas the same kind of woman in England would probably go for the "less is more" philosophy.

You only have to see them at weddings, the ultimate opportunity for dressing up, to understand what I'm getting at. These days English women look at their most elegant on such occasions, with hats and lovely flowing dresses. (Though I must admit, some still don't know how to wear a hat properly. It should be flat on the head instead of tilted on the crown "to frame the face.") Italian women old enough to know better will wear mini skirts and impossibly high heeled shoes which make their leg muscles look like gnarled trees. It only serves to make them look as if they're trying hard to maintain the "stay young and beautiful" mantra, "because they're worth it." This lack of sartorial independence, wearing the latest thing no matter whether it suits or not, saddens me because, as you must know by now, I love Italians and hate to sound critical.

Women presenters on Italian TV all have identical hairstyles. You know the sort of thing: long, artfully curled and very shiny. They play with it constantly, flicking it back or tucking it behind an ear.

Best of all are the four *professoressas* who star in a nightly quiz show called *L'Eredita*. The host is Carlo Conti, an amiable man with an amazingly kippered face, who asks the questions. When the contestants get something wrong, one of the *professoressas* will read the answer and an explanation from a card, simpering whilst doing so, to show her highly glossed lips to advantage. Italian friends I've spoken to about this show all see nothing wrong with these admittedly beautiful young women flaunting themselves on the set. They protest that they are all graduates and are displaying their intelligence. My feeling is that if they're so intelligent, why do they demean themselves by performing in that way? I bet the brightest graduate of their year wouldn't be on the show if she had a squint, or if she had bulges in the wrong places. Half way through the hour-long show comes the time for "*La Scossa*" (the shock). One of the girlies will wiggle her way to the centre, accompanied by striptease music, and perform a choreographed series of titillating movements, usually ending with her swishing her hair forward over her face, then back, and pouting in close-up. The quiz continues, then just in case all the questions are getting a bit too tedious, we have a short dance performed by all the *professoressas,* dressed in identical skimpy outfits. They dance to a piece of pop music, in what can only be described as pole dance style, but without the pole. Carlo claps admiringly when it ends, the live audience cheers, and we return to the quiz once more. No wonder people look benignly on Berlusconi's dalliances. They're part of the culture.

The break for adverts during *L'Eredita* offers another surprise. As well as the usual sales pitches and jingles for *telefoninos* or shampoo, who do we see but the bronzed Carlo and the *professoressas* advertising some product with scripted enthusiasm. Currently, it's mattresses, but around Christmas time they were enthusing about slippers (unlikely) and a healthy yoghurt drink. Observe Carlo closely and you might detect a difference in his tan, as these commercials are clearly recorded. He's often pale when waxing lyrical about fitted kitchens, then becomes suddenly very bronzed again when we see him with the next round of contestants.

He recently had his first black contestant on L'Eredita. Carlo congratulated the man on being the first on the show to be darker than he was. At least he's willing to send himself up.

But if I sound complaining, I'm not. I enjoy this programme because all the questions are written like sub titles, so I can read them and try to respond from the multiple choice answers. It's a great boost if I can answer correctly when Italians can't, but it's always entertaining watching kippered Carlo and the erudite pole dancers, and I admire them for working hard, and doing the show six nights a week, a programme lasting over an hour.

Italian day time television is naturally dominated by cookery programmes. The difference between theirs and ours is that it's the food which is the celebrity and not the chef. There is however an equivalent of the Domestic Goddess who even looks like Nigella, but the Italian version doesn't do any cooking. She stands attractively next to a real chef, usually male, who makes a dish explaining things as he goes along. She breathlessly asks the occasional naïve questions, but her real purpose is demonstrated when the final product comes out of the oven. Her role is to be seduced by the food. She sighs and exclaims at the presentation, and nearly faints in ecstasy when she tastes it. The mmms and the ahhhs with closed eyes and glossy parted lips in close-up leave little to the imagination. Each half hour programme will have half a dozen chefs and as many dishes. Her remarkable ability to reach multiple orgasms rivals or exceeds Meg Ryan's.

The adverts on Italian TV always amuse me. I'm sure a greater proportion of time is given to food than on our commercial channels, and the female body is used to sell just about anything. It seems that using English gives a product a certain cachet. Words such as "technology" and "beautiful" are frequently dropped into the sales pitch, and there are often mysterious slogans in English. What on earth does "Life is now" mean? (It's an advert for Vodaphone.) I can sort of see what Renault's slogan is getting at with "Drive the Change," but it's not quite right.

The news offers further examples of strange English. They like to talk about *"il think tank"* but pronounce it "tink tank". Then there are odd adaptations of English like *il tutoreggio* or *lo start up.* Football commentaries talk about *il standing ovation* and *il corner.* They use the word *killer* quite a lot in the news. The plural is also *il killer.*

My favourite quiz programme *L'Eredita* recently asked contestants what the word *bovindo* meant, suggesting it had an English derivation. I couldn't begin to guess what it might be, but we were informed that it meant a bow window. Sure enough, I looked it up in my big dictionary, and it's there, though Italian friends didn't recognise the word.

But nothing is as good as the weird English of tee shirts, or bizarre information for tourists.

Italian markets are always a pleasure to wander round, with their sounds, smells and bright colours of all the fresh food on display. I used to be less interested in the clothing stalls, but now I zoom in on them, notebook at the ready. It's actually quite difficult to find a tee shirt or pair of child's pyjamas with anything written in Italian on it. English is the language of choice; no matter that it usually doesn't make any sense at all to those of us who actually speak the language.

Sometimes you can see what the slogan writer was getting at.

Be meek when you're big like me

I suppose would be modestly worn by someone's little man, but a cute small girl who likes *My Little Pony* would not be happy to wear a slogan like

Sweet Little Horse

if she lived in England. Nor would a little boy all ready for bed be best pleased with the slogan underneath the decoration of a washing line on his pyjama top which simply says

Hung Down.

Sometimes the writing is just plain stupid.

If you prove imagine the rainbow you would have light passion

or

Choose music dreams star

are nonsense; random words strung together. There are many examples like this: I have a note book full, and they give a purpose to my shopping trips in markets.

Almost as good is the kind of thing they write for us English tourists to help us, as we don't speak their language. I was looking in a guide book about the best places to eat and stay in Umbria and came across this little gem.

> "…chefs are able to cuddle the gourmets with international and regional menus."

I know I've said all along how friendly Italians are, but I've never been offered a cuddle by an Italian chef.

Slightly scary was the advertisement I spotted for accommodation which referred to *Il Paradiso Bad and Breakfast: our porpuse is your pleasure.* It prompted the ever-sardonic Phil to remark in Star Trek speak: "It's English, Jim, but not as we know it."

Foreign brand names are another source of amusement. Over recent years I have never returned from Spain without a few packets of *Bonky* coffee. In Germany you can buy *Bum* talcum powder, and in Portugal *Ponce* soap is always on my shopping list. Italy, disappointingly, doesn't have much to offer on that front, though I've combed the supermarkets. I always buy *Il Capitano* toothpaste because I like the image on the packet, and I love the brand name *Smacchio* which is their equivalent of *Vanish*, for getting rid of stains. On the other hand, calling a brand of sausages *Wudy* doesn't encourage me to buy. The elusive but highly collectable *Rio Bumbum* washing up liquid is particularly prized, but I've only seen it in Sardinia.

There's a local removal company in Montebello which has the name *Self Control Removals* in English on the side of its van. It makes me think of your average removal company going berserk with all the boxes and furniture, whilst our local lads remain calm in adversity. I infer though that they're trying to give the impression that the customer is in charge and every wish is catered for.

Rome these days is covered in graffiti, much of it in mangled English. From the airport bus, I spent several minutes working out what was meant by *bax banni,* written in that large "bubble writing" you see everywhere. It dawned on me later that the writer meant Bugs Bunny.

But I think my all-time favourite example of strange language has to be the semi-official sign I spotted in Venice near the Rialto Bridge where often you get people selling fake designer goods arranged on sheets on the pavement.

When buying bad bag you may also be fined

This warning is so impressive that it has inspired me to call my whole collection of mangled English *The Bad Bag Collection*. (All contributions welcome.)

12. "BUT WE WERE ON YOUR SIDE... EVENTUALLY." Eccentric villas, castles and museums

The Veneto is Palladio country. There are villas by Palladio and his followers dotted all over the countryside, from the breathtakingly beautiful Villa Maser (in the province of Treviso) to the rather shabby ones where owners can't really afford the upkeep, but you can ring up and visit for a small charge. I like these eccentric places.

You can't miss the Villa Miari when you arrive at Sant' Elena: its ancient brick walls line one side of the main street. Beyond are glimpses of the upper storey, once stuccoed and painted in geometric patterns in terracotta and cream. Now, huge chunks have fallen off, exposing crumbling brickwork. The guide book describes its frescoed rooms and rare eighteenth century library in glowing terms, hardly preparing you for the reality.

Of course faded grandeur has its charm, and we went through the gate keen to see inside.

A squadron of small yapping dogs rushed to greet us as we crunched across the gravel to what appeared to be the entrance. Discarded toys and a plastic push-along *carabinieri* car littered the unkempt lawn, and a small hand-written *biglietteria* sign was propped up on a rusty iron table near a door with panes of broken glass mended with duct tape. The door, however, was locked.

As usually happens in Italy, we were being watched through

the gate by a local. When we failed to get in, he scurried towards us to be of service, shooing away the dogs and muttering something about the *campanello.* Of course the doorbell wasn't working. He banged on the door, calling for someone, and eventually an elderly man with long grey hair and buck teeth, wearing a Barbour jacket, emerged, told us to wait a minute, and went back inside locking the door. Some five minutes later another door opened and he beckoned us inside, speaking to us in very bad German. (They always assume in this area that anyone foreign-looking must be German.) The wine on his breath was enough to make me stagger backwards. I assume he'd been deep into a lengthy siesta when we arrived, and was still rather unsteady – maybe because he was half asleep, but more probably because he'd consumed a vast amount of the local *vino.* We made it clear that we were *inglesi* but he carried on with an explanation about the villa half in Italian and half in German. I've come to realise that for many locals, any foreign language will do for every nationality. All tourists are the same.

The rooms were very gloomy and curiously furnished, becoming increasingly scruffy as we explored further. Planks of wood were propped up next to old empty picture frames, and a heap of metal trunks was gathering dust at the side of the billiard room. The library turned out to be small and dark. Its musty leather-bound books had taken over corridors and the edges of rooms in small dusty piles. I had the impression that someone had begun sorting them out about 70 years ago, then abandoned the project.

Rather like Venetian *palazzi* where the ground floors have been abandoned to seasonal floods, leaving the occupants to live on the upper floors, this villa's main rooms were clearly unoccupied by the family, but left to the ravages of time. We picked our way through the detritus to where our guide was trying to stay awake long enough to point us in the direction of the garden, along a path marked *privato*.

We first walked round the villa to see the main façade. The patchy patterned stucco with a crenellated top extended to a lower level which had probably once been an orangery. In a niche a bust of Dante stared disapprovingly ahead, paired with a satellite dish in the niche on the other side. The orangery had given up the battle with nature. Plants were sprouting in all directions through the walls and floor, and creepers hung from the ceiling forming a dense green curtain which parted in one place to reveal the mounted stuffed head of a stag.

The mangy garden with box hedges running wild might have once been rather lovely. As we surveyed it, something white moved on the other side of a hedge. We were not a little surprised to discover that it was a white horse, but in that context it should have been a unicorn, as in a painting by de Chirico. At least that explained the occasional piles of manure we subsequently came across on the lawn.

To the east of the villa was a large informal park, very much gone to seed, and a lake. Next to the tumbledown ice house stood a couple of concrete bunkers which served as public conveniences. They were squatties, of course, and the doors hung open revealing crowds of flies buzzing round the hole in the ground. Phil is often overcome by calls of nature, but here he preferred to water a tree.

* * *

In complete contrast to this decayed grandeur, the Villa

Widmann a few miles away is proudly maintained by the Borletti family (of kitchen equipment fame) and condescends to open its park to visitors on, and only on, Thursday afternoons. We strolled through the arch into the courtyard where the only person in sight was an athletic-looking woman wearing a pigeon on her head, and surrounded by a posse of ducks. As we approached, she swiped the pigeon off her head, but it kept within a safe distance ready to return to its perch. I asked, somewhat doubtfully whether we could see the gardens, but there was no problem. She shooed away the ducks and picked up an enormous iron key.

Inside the archway was an ancient oak door leading to a stone staircase. At the top was one of the most amazing spaces I've ever seen: an immense old granary with a wavy brick floor and sturdy 16th century rafters. Once a year they hold a Slow Food feast here for 900 people. (Memo to self. Got to go next year.) Our guide explained that there had been a wooden floor over the bricks in earlier times, but the *vigili del fuoco* (fire brigade) insisted it had to be removed as a fire hazard. Underneath, some wheat grains had fallen through the floorboards and were found to be old varieties no longer used. They've succeeded in germinating these seeds so that flour can once again be made from traditional varieties.

This theme continues throughout the grounds. They grow vines in the traditional way, festooned across gaps between small trees, and produce a very unusual wine, *friularo,* which was used by the Venetians for their ships because it was known to travel well. The orchard is filled with rare peach and pear trees, and their chickens, clearly the friends of our guide with a live pigeon hat, are the strange punk-like birds of the Padovan breed with spiky manes around their heads. She calls them her *ragazzi* (children) and feeds them with fallen peaches.

The ecological perfection of the estate can only be marvelled at. There are hares running along the avenues of the vineyard, the trees and bushes have all been chosen for rare varieties of birds and there are acres of unpolluted meadowland for butterflies.

The formal garden contains a marvel of a different kind. Here, there is a cluster of statues of Goldoni characters. (He performed his plays in the villa's theatre.) On summer evenings they have a sort of son-et-lumiere show where spotlights fall on these statues in turn and they "speak". The trouble is, it's in Venetian dialect, but I rather think their November Wine Festival might be worth a visit. Tasting is a universal language.

* * *

When you come upon a fine 13th century castle in the middle of nowhere, standing in a well cared-for garden, the last thing you expect to find in a beautiful rose bed is a rusting helicopter. Along the winding paths you then encounter rocket launchers, and a sea plane floating in the middle of a lily pond. A plane seems to have flown half way though the vast solid castle walls and got stuck. This is our local Museum of the Air, the sort of eccentric museum I love.

One fine September day we arrived in the car park to find a handful of men in uniform unfurling flags and pulling on their gauntlets. Curious, I went across to ask what they were up to.

"It's an important anniversary for our air force, signora. Could we ask what nationality you are?"

The response on finding we were English was, "We were on your side... eventually." Hand shakes all round.

I suppose they'd have tailored the reply differently if they'd encountered German tourists.

They were gathering for a reunion lunch in the castle whilst we were wandering around the building and gardens, the only visitors, marvelling at the craziness of it all.

Anything remotely to do with flight has been lovingly collected and displayed. Whole planes hang from beamed ceilings inside the castle and along the loggia. Old photographs of early flights adorn the walls. A large cobwebby room with a very uneven floor contains twenty or more meticulously-made models of aircraft, each resting on its own shabby Persian rug. You come across crazy inventions such as a 19th century winged bicycle propped up in a corner next to interpretations of Leonardo's flying machines. One room contains sheet music from two world wars. If it has a picture of a Spitfire or a Messerschmidt on the cover, it is part of the collection.

This room leads directly into the ballroom. There are the usual faded frescoes on walls and ceiling, and several tarnished mirrors which have seen better days; but you hardly expect to see four hot air balloons suspended from the ceiling. Better still, if you stand in a certain position they are reflected over and over again, a shoal of floating Montgolfiers jostling for position and waiting to be released into the sky.

Every rickety staircase in the castle has a parachute hanging down the stairwell. There are different designs which serve different purposes like, for example, the parachutes used to slow down a fighter plane when landing on an aircraft carrier. That took some working out. Of course none of the information is in English. In fact, it's hardly possible to read the Italian either because the ink on the handwritten cards is so faded. At the bottom of the main staircase you meet an ejector seat with half a pilot sitting in it. He rather reminded me of my early attempts to make a Guy Fawkes out of old clothes and newspapers, but perhaps he is intended to look seriously injured.

On the first floor various rooms have been arranged to show important moments in flight history. There's the Red Baron, of course, leaning casually against a rather fine marble fireplace, as well as RAF and Italian pilots in original uniforms ready to scramble at a moment's notice.

In fact, these frozen moments in time in the rooms of the castle gave me an idea. Hanging neglected in a wardrobe is my father's R.A.F. demob overcoat, issued in 1945. My sons both tried wearing it, but it was far too heavy for your average trendy man about town. I realised that the Air Museum might be the perfect home for the treasured coat. It would be cared for, would no longer take up too much space in my cupboard, and I'd be giving something back to the local community.

I approached the signora who seemed to be in charge, bustling about setting tables for the airman's reunion lunch. She was delighted. I'm to bring it next time we travel to Italy by car (far too heavy to carry in luggage) and I will then receive free entry to the museum for life. A good deal. But back to the exhibits.

At the end of the corridor is the *piece de resistance.* It was from this very place that Gabriele D'Annunzio, famous Italian poet and pilot, planned the daring sortie over Vienna in the First World War. They dropped leaflets over the city, to prove that had they wanted, they could have dropped bombs. We see in a room D'Annunzio's rather moth-eaten wax work team, sitting round an oval table planning their mission, with the maestro himself looking distinguished in his eye patch, leading the discussion. Elsewhere there are bits of his aeroplane, his medals, and even one of his girlfriends' shoes. He had eight mistresses all together, most of whom remained attached to him for life.

Poignant, maybe. Crazy, certainly.

* * *

The little town of Monselice clusters itself around a volcanic cone a little separated from the others. On top, of course, is a ruined castle, but there's a better-preserved one a little way up the hill. I like this castle. It's not so crumbling that it would be impossible to live there. It has a romantic "Juliet" balcony where the custodian is wont to give impromptu recitations of Shakespeare in Italian, and the music room has stuccoed walls painted in a checkerboard of cream and terracotta. Because it's so well-preserved it's often used for filming, and immense silver pantechnicons squeeze up the cobbled street to unload vast quantities of equipment and props.

I was recently there with a friend one lunchtime when all the crew and cast had clearly decided that a meal was far more important than guarding the piles of cables, tripods, scaffolding and assorted suits of armour scattered all around. We amused ourselves trying on crowns and sitting on mediaeval x-shaped thrones whilst snooping about. No one chased us away so we grew bolder, hunting through boxes of iron candlesticks and fire irons for anything interesting and unusual. All the props were genuine, as far as I could tell, and not the sort of fakey things you imagine might be used in films.

Instinctively as the various clocks of Monselice struck 3 over the next 10 minutes, we tidied everything away assuming they'd be back, and wandered up the *viale delle sette chiese*. This lovely little lane is guarded by two lions on top of pillars looking at each other, one rather sadly, and one, wearing on his head a cross between a crown and a Venetian chimney, grimacing and baring its teeth, perhaps because he's lost a paw.

The seven chapels each contain a large but not very good oil painting, and are painted brilliant white and yellow, spaced at regular intervals leading to Villa Duodo. This villa has its own rather more special chapel, cared for by an over-friendly gentleman who rather likes to fondle female tourists, of whom there are not very many. He tries to entice them into the sacristy to buy the sort of tacky souvenirs you might win at a fairground "for the upkeep of the chapel."

Better to avoid the sacristy altogether and walk straight through to the main altar where a strange sight awaits. Arranged on shelves in a semi-circle are dozens of diminutive skeletons dressed in 17th and 18th century costumes apart from their exposed skulls. They're all labelled, with prominence given to the central little skeleton, clad in red velvet and

127

identified as St. Valentine. Seeing this, I remembered that his presence is used as an excuse for a great *festa* in Monselice on February 14th.

My friend and I discussed this rather macabre display.

"Were they all children?" she wanted to know.

Reluctant as I was to make contact with the *donnaiolo* custodian with a penchant for the ladies, I went into the sacristy to ask that very question. His answer was curious and illuminating.

He explained how the skeletons were all bought by the owner of the grand villa at the time of the clearing of the catacombs in Rome. Aristocrats readily assumed that these were the bones of Christian martyrs, and could be venerated as saints. Buying a job lot for decent burial could guarantee them their entry to Paradise. Our particular local grandee had decided to build only a small chapel, but had acquired rather a lot of skeletons. His solution was simply to use the upper bodies, the feet and the skulls, and throw the leg bones away, making them much shorter, with space for more saintly occupants along the shelves.

"But what about St. Valentine?" we asked in chorus, rather disappointed.

"Well, *signore*," he replied, tapping his nose. "Perhaps it is, and perhaps it isn't, but we in Monselice believe that St. Valentine rests here."

13. VENICE: the world's largest floating cocktail party

In mid-February the direct trains from Montebello to Venice carry a different kind of passenger. Not so much from Montebello itself, where the locals are suspicious of such frivolity, but along the platforms of Montegrotto and Abano which you pass through on the way to Padua, then in the bustle of Padua itself, gaudily clad tourists and Italian youngsters pile into the trains for the Venice carnival.

There are the usual ghastly felt jesters' hats with bells on each peak, and the more sober tricorns favoured by older Germans. The women wear masks with feathers and sequins, and long velvet cloaks, but they are as nothing compared with the stunning ensembles of the Venetians themselves.

At the end of every alley way, on the steps of every small bridge, there will be a group of 18th century aristocrats poised frozen in time for the photographs of voracious tourists. I suspect that many Venetians are professional 18th century people, always living in their Rococo past and perfecting their wigs, buckles, satin waistcoats and fans for their next outing.

Over the centuries, Venice has been fortunate in having though its trading connections wonderful silks and brocades for the fine clothes of its inhabitants. The Palazzo Fortuny was the home of a Spaniard who created the distinctive pleated silks which bear his name. There's a rather odd story about how Fortuny came to be based in Venice in the 19th century when he'd been living in Paris, the obvious place, you'd think, for a designer. His problem was, the poor man, that he was afraid of horses, but he managed in an age of horse-driven traffic to find a solution. All commercial cities in the world bar one had transport systems based on the horse. Venice, of course has a system based on water: in fact, horses were banned. So he lived, worked and achieved world-wide recognition there, and his dark, slightly dilapidated palazzo is worth a visit for time-travelling into an era of art nouveau, early photography and rich wall hangings, and for a glorious view of fantastically shaped chimney pots from the top floor.

It came to me as a blinding flash of revelation some years ago that *carne vale* means "goodbye to meat", the last bash before the privations of Lent. So as well as an orgy of ostentatious costume, eating and drinking to excess have a great part to play. The theme of the most recent carnival was the senses: if you had any sense you made a beeline for the *sestiere* which had taste as its theme. Every piazza (or *campo* as they are known in Venice) had stalls where they handed out mulled wine together with the special cakes only made at carnival time. *Fritelle* are rather like doughnuts, ping-pong sized balls, often filled with *crema* or *zabaglione*. (The latter are definitely the best.) *Galani* are thin crisp layers of deep fried pastry dredged with icing sugar, rather like a brittle sweet *lasagna*. Gorging on these delicacies, we found ourselves in a group of other gourmets comprising Napoleon, a prisoner with a ball and chain, and several furry animals. The cakes were being handed round by a figure wearing four masks, one for each point of the compass, and an ankle-length flowing robe. It was impossible to tell which way he was facing, apart from the way his arms emerged with the tray.

And of course all this takes place in deepest winter. The

mist hangs along the canals with icicles suspended from the bridges, and the gondoliers plough their silent way along the leaden waters huddled up in their navy reefer jackets against the cold, their boats curled like giant black Moroccan slippers. The city is at its most mysterious and beautiful at this time, as if the 21st century is yet to arrive.

But it arrives with a bang once every two years for the Biennale. Despite feeling that it's all a big con trick, I have to admit that I rather enjoy this amazing extravaganza. Not for nothing is Venice known by the media hangers-on as the world's biggest floating cocktail party.

For a start, it's always an impressive beginning to any day out to take the world's best and cheapest sightseeing cruise all the way down the Grand Canal on the number one *vaporetto* and get off at Giardini where it feels a different world, a municipal park with no canals and alleyways. There was even a zoo here once, where Robert Browning used to enjoy feeding an elephant. It's normally peaceful, except of course when the art jamboree comes to town every other year.

You walk through the park to barriers and a row of temporary huts selling tickets. The first shock is the price. It costs around 18 euros per person, but it's worth paying up for the entertainment value if not for the art. The people queuing for tickets tend to be young-ish, (say, under 40) earnest-looking, with a preponderance of Germans. They put on their serious "I'm looking at great art" faces, and it never occurs to them to question the merits of the work on display. Obedience is all: these are the cutting edge people, the politically correct, the greens, the save-the-planet tribe.

Their uniform is black, they carry their accessory bottles of water, and they are very serious.

Actually, it's worth knowing how to avoid the annoying wait to buy a ticket at the Giardini. It's always the same: crowds of people waiting and only three windows open. Once they reach the front of the queue, they never consider those still waiting, but start conversations about what's on offer. And of course Italians are not well known for queuing. Patient Brits need to be assertive in this climate if they want to get in before midday. Far better to walk along to the Arsenale, the alternative main site, where there are ticket booths with no queues. It's a quieter site which is stunningly beautiful; more so than the art, but we'll come to that later.

Patriots make for the British pavilion first. Four years ago it contained heaps of sticks by Tracey Emin who was also the only artist *selling* little leaflets about her work. (Others gave them away, and the Americans had heaps of A3 prints up for grabs every day.) In 2005 Gilbert and George peered solemnly down at us from huge enamel-bright slabs like stained glass windows featuring men in suits instead of saints. The most recent British offering was a film show which perhaps sent up the Biennale by showing the deserted Giardini site in winter, with puddles, litter, homosexual encounters, and stray dogs peeing on the pavilions. It set me wondering what happens to all the art. Does it end up in a skip? Cynics might say that's where it belongs anyway. I couldn't possibly comment.

Some pavilions are like stage sets. I remember a Scandinavian one which was like a crime scene, a modern open plan house with a body floating in the pool. The Czech one was just an empty space with an unkempt garden. Had they forgotten to make their contribution, or were we supposed to see profound meaning in a bunch of weeds? The gorgeous art nouveau Hungarian pavilion was filled in 2007 with quirky figures, several in old brass diving helmets. If it meant anything, it was lost on me, but I rather liked it.

Exhibitions often have enigmatic titles which are, when you begin to think about it, meaningless, like so much contemporary art. I don't see why it has to mean *anything*, but cutting edge young artists see themselves as political commentators (without much knowledge of politics) or philosophers (with definitely no sense of philosophy) because essentially, they can neither draw nor paint and they have to prove themselves in some way.

Think with the senses, feel with the mind was the title of the 2007 Biennale. It's nonsense, of course, but on the surface it sounds clever. It set the tone for many of the contributions in the various pavilions. The French one was particularly memorable. Sophie Calle, the artist, had, as women's magazines would put it, been "dumped". This might not have been so bad, but she was dumped by email, which obviously infuriated her. She sent copies to 30 of her female friends for their reactions, and these were the subject of the French show. Of course they all agreed that he was an unfeeling beast, and reacted according to their professions. His text was psychoanalysed, set to music, deconstructed, paraphrased. She sent it to a sexologist, a criminologist and even a blind woman. Typically, there were no translations of these letters which constituted the "art" and many bemused tourists wandered round not quite knowing what to make of it, the mind-set of the majority at the Biennale anyway.

What I wanted to know was, did her lover know what

she had done with his private message, and had he been outed. If he had, I imagine he'd be receiving hate mail by the sackful from feminists world wide. We were not told. Maybe we'll get another installment at a future Biennale, but there was nothing to continue the saga in France's more recent exhibition.

The other major site for the Biennale, the Arsenale, is pure pleasure. Notice I said the site and not the art. With one or two honourable exceptions, the art is the same old claptrap.

The Arsenale is an enclosed world where the greatest seafaring nation of its day overhauled and repaired ships, and provided the equipment they needed before setting sail. Usually much of the area is closed to the public, but the Biennale offers a great opportunity to see the cathedral-like vaulted warehouses and especially the Corderia, the rope-making building with its amazing long vista punctuated at intervals by brick columns. Generally the art which they put in these grand spaces detracts from their simple majesty, and this is not helped by the kind of pseudo-intellectual nonsense which is used to explain the exhibits. (Should art have to be explained?) Try this one for size, accompanying a Dutch offering:

"The emancipation realized at Position 3 results in an internalization of the potential of agency here, creating several positions not for speech but for thought. Here, action and awareness of action are not different. Because agency can only be actualized when there is a separation between an act and the awareness of this act, in this condition agency is destined to remain potential."

Falke Pisano

No comment.

However, as I say, the Arsenale itself is a delight. A little ferry shuttle takes you across the enclosed rectangle of water to the Spazio Thetis, the row of former warehouses on the other side, some still in dire need of restoration. At the last 2009 Biennale, one of them contained the top of a giant human head with a life-size figure digging a trench into the brain as if it were a first world war landscape. We observed it solemnly from a viewing platform.

Mostly what's on show in these enormous spaces is out of scale. Rows of flickering computer screens sit uneasily amongst ancient crumbling brickwork. But one warehouse providing the space for an Austrian sculptor had got it right. Here were enormous steel shapes by Bernar Venet, reminiscent of the work of Serra. They felt industrial, solid and immense, entirely in keeping with their surroundings.

But even with something spiritually uplifting as great art should be, it's good to escape the party atmosphere and wander back into the real Venice. The population of the city has halved in the past two decades, but life goes on much as it always has in the *calle* and *campi* off the well-worn track between the *Ferrovia* and San Marco. We always call at Torrefazione Marchi on the Strada Nova to buy ground coffee, and at our favourite hardware store, Ratti, to buy the odd useful item and remind ourselves that Venice isn't just a theme park but a living city.

It's curious how, when wandering around a place, questions suddenly come to you which you've previously accepted unquestioningly. In Venice there are no Venetian blinds. So why are they called Venetian blinds? The answer apparently lies in a type of heavy canvas called *rasse*, made in Venice and originally used to make canopies for gondolas. This canvas was known as "Venetian" in 18th century England, and was used to bind together the slats of blinds.

I love such trivia, and Venice proves a rich source. There is, for instance, a narrow walkway called, in rough translation, Titty Street. You might guess in trying to explain how it got its name, that it was in Venice's red light district, and you'd be partly right, but the real answer is much better. The ruling powers of Venice decreed that there were too many gay sailors frequenting the streets, and decided that the best way of putting a stop to such undesirable behaviour was to encourage young women to bare their breasts from upstairs windows to tempt the sailors back to heterosexuality.

The Venetian dialect is almost another language, and is still widely spoken. The clothes in the Museum of Textiles and Clothing, the Palazzo Mocenigo, are all labelled first in the dialect word because the new fashions were invented in Venice, so first named here. It's not surprising that Venetian dialect has the only known word for the reflection of water on a ceiling, *la vecia*. Poetic, like Venice itself.

For centuries Venetians were known as *pantaloni* (wearing trousers) but this may have originated from a corruption of *pianta leoni* (lion planters) because wherever they traded in the known world they "planted" their lion symbols, the winged lion being the symbol of St. Mark.

The Venetian lion appears in two distinct forms. One is as a winged animal resting on water, to symbolise dominance over the seas, holding the Gospel under a front paw. The other form, which I find much more interesting, is known as the lion "*in moleca*", in the form of a crab. (Readers with a good memory will remember the feast of soft shell crabs in the local trattoria in Montebello.) Here the lion is depicted full-faced with its wings circled around the head resembling the claws of a crustacean. It is emerging from water, so that the lion "*in moleca*" is associated with the lagoon and the city whereas the standing winged lion is thought to be more associated with Venetian territory around the Mediterranean.

Nowadays the delicately balanced ecology of the lagoon is being suffocated by the hordes of tourists who come to marvel at, or just to tick off, ("been there, done that") this unique city, La Serenissima. Cruise ships grow larger every year, and channels have to be dredged to allow them to dock. In taking away the mud which lies on the floor of the lagoon, they are removing the algae which help to preserve the poles on which the city is built. You could say that Venice is nailed to the seabed with millions of wooden nails hammered into the lagoon. Without protection, the wood rots and Venice's sinking is accelerated.

It was Venice that offered the first image of the tourist city playing host to innumerable pigeons, and just as in Trafalgar Square, Venetians are a bit sentimental about these birds in St Mark's. You'll never see pigeon on a Venetian menu even though 25 miles away in my territory they're a speciality. Some cafes throw crumbs to the lame or one-legged ones, but this sentimentality is only superficial.

We once caught the very early train to Venice and arrived at the entrance to the Museo Correr just as the silent trapping ritual was taking place. Several men holding a large net were walking across St Mark's shepherding the birds under the arches at the far end where we were watching. Here they flew straight into another net which was quickly covered with an enormous black cloth, so they became silent. The cloth and its contents were gathered up and put on a large trolley to be pulled away to where they would presumably be dispatched. Nobody talks about the pigeon cull, but there it is. I've seen it.

Taking a *vaporetto* from the Fondamente Nuove to one of the islands gets you away from the day trippers, though plenty of longer-stay tourists make the trip to Murano and Burano. We recently took some American friends out across the lagoon and were amused by their different reactions. Trish, my school pen friend (we're been writing to each other since we were both eight) was stunned by the colours and surfaces. Camera at the ready, she kept muttering "textures, textures" and seemed almost drunk on the experience.

Trish "won" me in a handwriting competition at her school in rural Iowa. I don't really think of myself as a prize. One single English pen friend was on offer for the whole class (I've no idea why that was me) and the teacher wisely decided to award me to the pupil with the most improved handwriting. Dear Trish must have put an amazing amount of effort in, because even today I can still hardly read her writing. We get on amazingly well given the randomness of how we came to know each other.

Terry meanwhile, her practical scientist husband, was noting all the engines on the moored motorboats.

"That's a Yamaha, that's a Johnson…."

As we returned with them on the train across the long causeway from Venice, I mused about the fierce independence of the Venetians which caused them to leave a space under every arch of the causeway for dynamite, should they ever again need to cut themselves off from the mainland. In contrast to the modern cult of personality, Venice cultivated impersonality. The individual was nothing, Venice everything. You still get a sense of that today, and I hope it continues.

14. NON-SLIP STONES FOR VENICE:
the story of Montebello's canal

I often wonder when Ruskin wrote his great work *The Stones of Venice* whether he knew where the stones actually came from and how they were transported there. The answer is, they came from "my" hills and were transported from "my" village across the lagoon to Venice.

Yes, in the sleepy faded spa town of Montebello lies the key to the building of the great and unique city of Venice. The area of volcanic cones and hot springs around Montebello is now a national park and an area favoured particularly by German tourists for its spa treatments and its wines. But at some point a thousand or more years ago it must have been discovered that the volcanic stone quarried there provided the perfect paving stones for the passages and alleyways of Venice, having a rough texture which prevented slipping, very important for a city based on water.

Canals provided the easiest means of transport to ship these stones to Venice and in consequence a network of navigation systems sprang up and remained in use until the mid 20th century. The main canal at Montebello, wide and free of weeds with wonderful wild flowers along its banks, was constructed between 1189 and 1201, preceding by several centuries the canals of the English Industrial Revolution. It was built at ground level with walls and banks to contain it, rather than dug out in trenches as our canals were.

A stroll at any weekend in the year in Montebello will usually take you along the canal, past snoozing fishermen and the occasional grandfather teaching his grandson the traditional way of rowing standing up. It's what they do after mass, or after lunch. There's a cycle track too, so the wide path can get quite busy, but no one's in a hurry. Like the *passeggiata*, you're there to see and be seen. In many ways this is the most important thoroughfare in Montebello. In winter, they sometimes have torch-lit canal side walks with pauses for readings at every lamp post, and the summer pageants always include trips along the canal with the central bridge as the starting point.

I used to wonder why the car park near the roundabout at the entrance to Montebello was always completely full at weekends, with no one in sight. Only recently have we begun to explore the hill behind the car park, and have discovered a warren of pleasant footpaths bordered with wild roses, curving and winding around the old quarries of Monte Ferro. Families come here at weekends for picnics and barbecues, or set up tents to wait for dusk and a spot of hunting. It's easy to see from here that half of Monte Ferro has disappeared, shipped along the canal from Montebello to Venice to be laid under the feet of countless generations of inhabitants and tourists.

The sheer rock face is divided into natural flat blocks which must have been comparatively easy to cut. Poppies and shrubs have found their way into the crevices, and the sheltered curve produces a micro-climate where prickly pears flourish. This peaceful scene must be an enormous contrast with the feverish stone-cutting of 800 years ago which created from a series of muddy islands the Venice we now recognise.

The most important festival in Venice is the annual wedding

ceremony when the city is symbolically married to the sea on which it depends. In recent years the enterprising folk of Montebello have copied Venice with a similar festival, marrying the village to its canal. The bride, Miss Montebello, is chosen by competition the day before. Almost the entire population gathers in the park in the evening, all dressed in mediaeval clothing. There are lords and ladies, clergy, drummers and trumpeters, oarsmen in fine velvet doublets and carrying their huge oars, and at the back, the peasants with their local produce. There's even a baby in a sort of ancient pram, a wooden wheelbarrow. The procession sets off, led by a splendid knight in armour on a white horse, and we all follow, round the side streets to the canal.

There, the "bishop" unrolls a scroll and reads, after a fanfare from the trumpets. As usual, it passes us by because it's in Venetian dialect, but luckily doesn't last long. Miss Montebello then tosses a wedding ring elegantly into the canal, and the procession leaves with much cheering and drumming, leaving the best bit until last. Silently in the dark, a fleet of rowing boats glides down the canal and under the bridge. The oarsmen have lit their boats with dozens of candles which flicker in the water, lending a magical atmosphere, with shimmering reflections mirroring the fireflies above.

The canal really comes to life at Christmas. Many Italian towns have a *presepio*, a crib, but Montebello's is a floating nativity scene. On a fleet of wooden rowing boats tied to wooden poles stand life-size figures depicting the story of Christ's birth. The first boat has Mary and Joseph under an awning with a crib, huddling over a realistic glowing fire. Shepherds and very life-like sheep float nearby, (the sheep are always made by the children of Montebello Primary

School) followed by a boat containing the wise men dressed in colourful silks and carrying their gifts. Other boats carry the representatives of Montebello with their traditional trades: knife-grinding, spinning, carpentry etc. They are all floodlit and form a remarkable sight from the Padua road: drivers often screech to a halt (this being Italy) to get a closer look.

Last year there was a huge outcry because someone stole the three kings and their gifts. Large indignant notices were stuck to the empty boat demanding that they should be returned because the scene meant so much to so many people. They never were. We await this Christmas's display with great anxiety.

Montebello's Museum of River Navigation has been the life's work (or at least the past 30 years) of the canal's last bargeman, my friend Riccardo Cappellozza. He tells the story of how he was chatting to his friend (and now mine) Federico the local librarian about his work as a barge man now that he was about to retire. They both realised that a whole language was about to disappear. Riccardo supplied the nouns for the tools and equipment, the verbs for the movement of cargo and business of sailing, and the stories about life on the barges, or *burci* as they are known locally. Federico recorded it all. From that small beginning, Riccardo began to collect the abandoned materials of his trade from whole boats to tiny hooks. The collection grew. Space was needed. Not everyone recognised the importance of all these objects, but some enlightened fellow citizens offered him the former abattoir to house the still-growing collection.

The SS16 Padua-Ferrara road follows this main canal, and the entrance to the little town of Montebello is across a modern bridge where various boats have been pulled up onto dry land, one eerily with a life-like figure keeping an eye on the traffic. This is the furthest outpost of the museum's collection, next to boat sheds where the canal widens to permit barges to be stored and brought out for the town's festive occasions, for rides to Catajo Castle and back for one euro. The museum itself is tucked away behind the main road, but could hardly be missed with its bright yellow walls and the assortment of anchors, mooring posts, buoys etc arranged in front of the entrance.

The museum shows the whole history of the almost forgotten world of river and lagoon transport, from the *squeri,* where the flat-bottomed barges were constructed (only one *squero* still remains in Venice itself, and that was brought back into use by an enthusiastic American), to the art of navigating the inland waterways. I love the fact that the son of Federico, Montebello's librarian, is the first apprentice at the newly reopened *squero* in Venice, San Trovaso, where gondolas are made again.

Last year Montebello's boat club was given a traditional wooden boat from Venice to repair. It was relaunched on the canal in September, after being liberally sprinkled with *prosecco,* and I was offered the first ride. Like the gondola it is asymmetrical, (have a look along the prow of a gondola some time and you'll see that there's a curve to correct the list caused by the weight of a single oarsman) and after a slightly wobbly ride, it was decided that some minor adjustments were necessary. It's now moored in the museum's boat house awaiting fine tuning.

To enter the Museum of Navigation is to time-travel to a gentler age of beautiful hand-crafted tools and a slower pace of life. There are, for example, several examples of the hand-carved *forcole,* receptacles for the oars made out of the hardest walnut, and beautiful pieces of sculpture in their own right. The last master carver still lives in retirement in a nearby village, and still occasionally makes new *forcole* in their traditional form, but these days from polished cherry wood. I'm the proud owner of a walnut *forcola*, offered to me for a modest sum by Riccardo when I'd helped the museum with a bit of publicity. It stands in my sitting room at home in Newcastle, a talking point about my other life in Italy.

As a child, Riccardo Cappellozza lived with his family on the barge for three summer months each year, trundling through the flat fertile landscape of a triangle formed by Mantua, Ferrara and Venice. There were paddle steamers then, like small versions of Mississippi steamboats, but his wooden barge, one of hundreds, was the common form of transport for the movement of all kinds of cargo, even after the advent of railways. (And he points out that today, with our awareness of energy conservation, canal transport is a much greener alternative to movement by road or rail. The canals are still there, and useable for more than the mere summer rides for tourists along the Brenta Canal to see Palladian villas.)

The museum's top floor gives the illusion that you're on a large barge. A ship's steering wheel with brass machinery faces directly onto the canal in front of a floor-length window, and all around are ropes, handling gear, oars and panniers. Riccardo has a great party trick with the ropes, one which he usually does for visiting school parties. With practised skill he quickly plaits and twists 20 foot lengths into knots and invites the children to undo them. When they don't succeed, he steps in and with a couple of deft flicks the ropes are straightened once more. The children are amazed, and Riccardo chuckles affectionately.

The freight boats of the canal and river systems of the Veneto were either wind-propelled, pulled by horses or pushed along by the boatmen themselves using long oars. Riccardo has even kept the harness which he himself used to pull the family barge along, before they could afford a horse. It was a hard life. A collection of domestic artefacts gives a picture of life on board. The family lived below deck where they kept wooden trunks for linens, a wood-burning stove for cooking and heating, a *moscheto* to keep insects away from food, and countless small utensils for every day use. The barge was home, as well as the means for getting to know the outside world which floated by. In it, the barge man passed through the basins and the *buta*, the flooding created artificially twice a week to compensate for the shallower parts of the navigation system.

Riccardo describes himself as a "water gypsy," always on the move, but encountering other gypsy friends at staging points along the trade routes. The water gypsies stick together and help each other out, as they always have. I met one of Riccardo's fellow gypsies recently when he decided to send me to meet him for a boat ride on the River Sile, just north of the Venetian Lagoon. We were met by Bruno Stefonato at Quartino Attesta where we had to follow him a few miles to park safely in his garden behind an electric fence. Then we were driven back again to board the boat. The amiable rotund Bruno wasn't the easiest person to understand, but he was clearly keen to make sure that we enjoyed our day on "the most beautiful river in the world." I'm not too sure about that claim. I think the world of the barge and river men perhaps only extends from the Italian border in the north, to the Apennines in the south. Still, the Sile is a pleasant smoothly flowing river, bordered by a few handsome villas, and now lined with trees which were not there in Bruno's youth because they would have obstructed the tow path. His old boat is now used for pleasure cruises, and we were joined by a noisy crowd from Trieste who arrived on a coach and bagged all the seats in the shade.

We'd been chugging along for only a matter of about 10 minutes when Bruno announced that it was time for apperitivi and antipasti. (It was by this time 10 o'clock.) Great jugs of *prosecco* appeared, along with baskets of *crostini* and hot crisp fish balls. The gannets from Trieste swooped, and kept an eye on our baskets in case there were any left. Nobody was remotely interested in the flora and fauna. We stopped at a small village a few miles upstream where a guide was to tell us a bit of local history. We listened dutifully for a while, but the combination of heat, *prosecco* and a very detailed delivery caused us to wander off back to the boat. I hadn't noticed before that the boat had quite a large kitchen at one end, and a team of three women was busy slicing calamari, sorting piles of prawns and stirring risotto in huge vats. Our lunch was being prepared. Afloat once more, Bruno reassured us that he would moor the boat during lunch the better to enjoy our feast. He loved talking with the microphone, and spent a lot of time telling jokes in dialect, which we didn't understand, but the atmosphere was very jolly.

Lunch time. More *prosecco*, of course, and bottled water, a fish risotto followed by *fritti misti* (an assortment of fried calamari and prawns) with salad, and lemon cake and coffee. The noise level reached epic proportions under the awning, and a few of the Trieste party began throwing bits of bread to the swans and coots, only to be reprimanded by others who wanted to consume the bread themselves.

At some point during the long hot afternoon, we began to wonder how we were going to get back to the car, as we'd travelled a long way upstream and were due to end the journey in Treviso. Bruno came to find us as everyone was disembarking.

"You'll have a chauffeur here in 20 minutes" was the gist of what he said.

We waited under a tree in the shade until he invited us back on board to meet the family, the next generation of water gypsies. There were two sons who waited at table, his wife in charge of the galley, and a daughter who worked behind the bar.

"Any friend of Riccardo Cappellozza is a friend of mine" said the genial Bruno, and offered yet more *prosecco* whilst we were waiting.

The chauffeur turned up. He was a 30-ish bear of a man with a growling voice we couldn't understand. Trustingly we got into his car which smelt powerfully of dog, and set off down the road. When we shot through the village where we'd left the car, we murmured politely, trying to conceal tones of concern.

"La macchina?"

The bear turned to us and growled something we didn't understand, so we carried on all the way back to the original departure point. There he got out and lit a cigarette, then went to have a conversation with the coach driver in the car park. We stayed put, as he gestured we should. Cigarettes extinguished, he returned to the car and we set off again back to pick up ours. I've no idea why we made this extra journey, but we were grateful eventually to find ourselves where we wanted to be.

We drove back along the *autostrada* to the *Colli Euganee*, thinking ourselves lucky it was Sunday so there weren't any large lorries to threaten us.

We'd only been back about five minutes when the bell rang. It was Riccardo, who must have been thinking about us all day, dying to know how the day had gone.

"*Tesoro!*" he exclaimed. (I like to be called his treasure.) "Was Bruno a good host? Did you enjoy your day?"

He always explains that his pleasure is to give pleasure to others, and we're lucky to be on the receiving end.

Riccardo Cappellozza's great achievement marking Montebello's important past has been recognised by the University of Padua which has awarded him an honorary degree, of which he is very proud. He is much more than a museum director; he is himself the most important exhibit in his museum, a vital connection with the artefacts of a way of life which no longer exists.

15. THE DAY I MET ROBERTO BENIGNI

The nearest city to Montebello is Padua, about 15 minutes on the train. It has the distinct advantage of not being a city besieged by tourists even in high summer, despite the attraction of the sublime Giotto frescoes in the Scrovegni Chapel.

Padua is known to Paduans as the city of

> The saint with no name,
> The meadow with no grass
> The coffee house with no doors.

No one refers to St Anthony of Padua because it's obvious: he's just "the saint." South of his basilica is an enormous piazza known as Prato (field) Della Valle. This is the meadow without grass. And Pedrocchi, the famous old café in the centre, part gothic, part classical in style, was always open 24 hours a day.

It's useful to have a city close-by for shopping trips, exhibitions and the theatre, and of course if you happen to need cheap household goods as I do for my little flat, there's always Ikea on the outskirts.

The Ikea in Padua is situated (conveniently from an Italian point of view) at the junction of the ring road (the *tangenziale*) and the Milan-Venice *autostrada*. As far as I'm concerned, this makes the trip to Ikea a nightmare. You can see the familiar blue and yellow building when you take the exit from the motorway, but once you've gone through the toll booths and paid, you then have to fight your way across several lanes of impatient drivers to find the small road leading to Ikea's car park.

Out most recent trip was to buy a tall cupboard to provide extra storage space. Phil was reluctant to take the wheel, but even more reluctant to navigate, so we set off in profound silence to aid concentration. By some miracle we made it to the car park first time instead of going round the system again, and made our way to the upper floor of furniture displays. I knew exactly what we needed, so I found a desk and ordered the parts with a confidence that proved to be unfounded.

"I'd like it to be delivered, please, in the next two weeks before we return to England."

"Ah no, signora. That's not possible. You have to give at least twenty days' notice for delivery."

"Oh dear. In that case, will you please deliver it in six weeks' time when we're here again?"

"That is too far ahead. You can only order furniture one month in advance."

The young man shook his head with some sympathy as I pulled a face of frustration, wondering when on earth it would be possible to get the cupboard.

"Bur, signora, it is very expensive in any case to have furniture delivered by Ikea. Why don't you simply collect what you want?"

He had to be told that we certainly couldn't carry a flat pack for a six and a half foot wardrobe on or in the Silver Snail.

"So you find a *ragazzo* (a lad) with a van. This will cost you less than our prices."

He beamed at me, pleased at having found a solution. I wondered who to ask in Montebello. Alberto the ancient handyman was not an obvious choice at his advanced age. In any case, I've only ever seen him on a bicycle. He may not have a van.

The answer came in the form of Dario, the young pony-tailed electrician with the lovely smile. He was fixing a light in the garage, which up to now had only had a "fatal flaw", a live wire coming from a hole in the ceiling. He agreed, and another aspect of life in Montebello was arranged to my satisfaction.

But back to Padua. Shopping there, as anywhere else in Italy, is a very different experience from our own shopping habits. First of all, it is important to realise that it will take time. Italians still like to shop in small specialist places, buying bread at the baker's, meat at the butcher's…. whereas we use supermarkets and zoom to the check-out as if our lives depend on it. Queuing in the Mercato Delle Erbe in Padua, I was quietly reflecting on this, at the same time aware that Phil was getting more and more agitated about the time it was taking. The woman in front of me was buying beetroots and courgette flowers, and inspected each one before asking for tomatoes. There followed a conversation about good recipes for beetroot before the all-important consideration of buying asparagus came up. It was the season for white asparagus, which can be bought in bundles with shoots of varying thickness. I'd have thought the thin shoots (which I prefer) would be cheaper, but no. Thick ones command up to 5.50 euros a bundle. I was consulted in the general conversation about quality and favourite recipes. I modestly and tactfully said I preferred to hear *their* recipes which of course extended the whole purchasing business for another 10 minutes.

By this time Phil looked as if he was going to do a war dance, so I suggested we wandered back towards the university and sat in a café to relax for a while.

Padua is an old university city, the Italian equivalent of Cambridge, being Italy's second oldest university after Bologna. It's always lively, with good cheap eating places and a youthful atmosphere. There's always plenty of entertainment to watch from the tables of a pavement café.

If you sit at a table and close your eyes, the sounds could only be Italy… hubbub and rattling china echoing under arcades, the occasional thudding slam dunk of emptying coffee grounds from an espresso machine, and a lone violinist, a busker playing Mozart, poignantly floating through the warm air.

But in Padua you need to open your eyes for the entertainment. Graduation ceremonies seem to happen throughout the year, and they involve the new graduates subjecting themselves to every possible humiliation. First you see the large posters, each with a caricature of the student displaying enhanced sexual characteristics. Around the drawing will be acres of small print delving into his or her notorious past, together with photos in compromising circumstances. There may be bawdy poetry, but very little to do with academic prowess.

The new graduates wear a variety of fancy dress. Babies wearing nappies is a popular choice. They choose a plinth to stand on, or maybe a bench in the city centre, and give speeches which are enthusiastically heckled. At the same time they are expected to consume vast amounts of alcohol, sometimes directly fed via a tube from a large container on their backs. Meanwhile, proud or embarrassed parents watch from a distance waiting to take them out for a more sedate celebration.

An honorary degree from Padua University is of course highly prestigious, a rather more sedate affair. Riccardo from the Museum of Navigation has received such recognition, as I've already said, and is rightly proud of it.

A few years ago we arrived in the city centre where crowds of excited students had assembled around the broad pedestrian area in front of the University. Police were manning the side streets and not allowing traffic through. (Italian policewomen often amuse me. They of course won't surrender their flowing locks or their high heeled shoes for work, and look ridiculous to English eyes with a long mane of corkscrew curls under a cap.)

I asked what was happening, to be told that Roberto Benigni, perhaps Italy's most popular film star, was to be awarded an honorary degree and they were hoping to see him. Now I'm on the small side and can never see over the heads of a crowd, so I decided it was rather pointless waiting where we were. I moved off down the side street where a would-be glamorous policewoman was directing traffic, tottering about on stilettos and blowing her whistle with authority. Everyone else clustered around the main entrance. After a while, at a signal to her earpiece, she stopped all the traffic and a solitary rather ordinary black car came slowly towards me, stopping between me and a narrow door. Out jumped two burly men who stood on either side of the car's rear door as Roberto Benigni himself stepped out right in front of me.

"Hello, Roberto," I said rather stupidly in English, in complete surprise.

"Hello," said Roberto Benigni, flashing me his famous idiotic grin.

To left and right I heard screams and pounding footsteps as hundreds of students rushed to greet him. Soon he and I were surrounded by people clamouring for autographs. There was no escape, so I stayed with him enjoying my vicarious fame. Several autograph books were thrust under my nose, but I politely and modestly declined. His body guards allowed about five minutes, then held back the crowds to let him go through the door. For a moment I thought I was to be marshalled inside with him, but they realised my insignificance and abandoned me.

"Goodbye, Roberto," I said.

"Goodbye," said Roberto Benigni, shrugging his shoulders as if to say "What can I do? I've got to go."

Anything else that day was going to be an anti-climax. I found my way back to Phil who had no idea about my brief flirtation with Italian cinema.

Telling my story to friends in Montebello the following day,

Silvia had another anecdote to add about my new friend Roberto.

Her niece is a dentist, and a well-known violinist is one of her patients. He sent her a ticket for a concert in Rome to which a lot of VIPs had been invited. Napolitano, the President of Italy, was sitting two rows in front of her. Just before the concert began, there was a bit of a commotion. Roberto Benigni clambered over several rows of seats to greet the President, then sat down to enjoy the music. Afterwards, to her surprise, the actor turned up in the violinist's dressing room, as he was a personal friend. When they were introduced, Benigni covered his mouth, saying "Don't look at my teeth!" (He is, I have to say, a bit "goofy.")

We agreed what a nice man he is, and how much Italy owes him. Personally. I don't much like the film he's best known for in the English-speaking world, *La Vita e Bella*. I find it comical in places where it ought to be harrowing. Nevertheless, Italians – and I – are all in admiration of his Dante marathon, reading the whole oeuvre on TV in prime time. (Rather like the equivalent of Kenneth Branagh reading the whole of Shakespeare every evening for several weeks.) That is why he was awarded his honorary degree, and that is why he is loved and revered in Italy. And by me.

AND THEN.......

It's late November. The last golden and red stripes in the vineyards are slowly fading away to leave the black skeletal shapes of the vines marching in rows across the landscape.

Another year in Montebello draws to a close, with renewed friendships, new acquaintances, new discoveries and many happy days of *dolce far niente.*

We're packing the car, the Silver Snail, for the return journey to England. With the back seats flat, we can fit in several cases of local wine as well as *panettone* and other goodies for Christmas. As we pass the row of garages carrying bags and boxes, there sits Sergio putting the finishing touches to a dog-sized reindeer made from wire coat hangers. He's painted it red and is twisting fairy lights all around its body. He wants us to wait for a demonstration and plugs it in. The lights flash on and off, red and green. It will stand outside guarding our block of flats at Christmas whilst we're away.

A last look around, and we close the shutters. Word will quickly get round that we've left. Just as when we arrive, the open shutters are a sign of occupancy and we get our first visitors within an hour, offering bread, tomatoes and gossip, they will now all be at the *Bar Centrale* exchanging the information that we've left, and wondering when we'll return.

We drive down via Cavour and spot Roberta shaking a rug on her balcony. She waves, rather triumphantly, then rushes inside. She will be able to carry the news that she saw us leave at 10am precisely.

We drive out of the village across the canal. A cluster of people with boxes, piles of material, figures and imitation life-size sheep are cleaning and varnishing a small fleet of rowing boats. They're preparing for the floating nativity which this year we won't see, but it's reassuring to know it'll still be there.

On past the cemetery, with a shudder of recollection as we pass the hire depot with its queues of diggers and cement mixers waiting to be hired, alongside a certain minibus with darkened windows and giant wing mirrors.

The next turn takes us to the *autostrada* where you have to pay for the privilege of risking life and limb to drive with menacing container lorries, or cars whose drivers never seem to realise that you too are moving as they overtake, and cut in front of you so quickly you have to brake. Often the stress is too great and we decide to take the ordinary roads, but they're very slow and there too there are risks and dangers when you factor in all the tractors and *api*. But we slowly leave the enclosed little world of volcanic hills behind us, and head north, already planning our return.

Acknowledgements

I wish to thank all my many friends in the Euganean Hills, and in particular Riccardo Pergolis and Sandra Romano without whose kind friendship and support I should be considerably more perplexed about Italian life.

Fabio and Manuela Piovan helped to make living in Italy a reality, and have been endlessly patient with my bad Italian. I would also like to acknowledge the inspiration and kindness of the late Mrs. Chris Fleming, and the thoughtful advice of Geoff Hare. My Italian class under the enthusiastic leadership of Annarosa Lazzaro has inspired confidence and always lent support.

I'm also deeply grateful to my mother, Doris Woodhead, who has accepted my constant comings and goings to Italy with good grace and never selfishly demanded that I should spend more time at home when she cannot travel.

Finally, my thanks go to Bill, constant companion and critic, who has listened patiently to the many drafts and has lived through many of the adventures on these pages.

Lightning Source UK Ltd.
Milton Keynes UK
17 March 2011

169462UK00001B/20/P